Hotel Security & Executive Protection

Hotel Security & Executive Protection

Editor
R K Sinha

Vitasta
Let Knowledge Spread

Published by
Vitasta Publishing Pvt. Ltd.
2/15, Ansari Road, Daryaganj,
New Delhi - 110 002
info@vitastapublishing.com

Hotel Security & Executive Protection
ISBN: 978-93-808-2819-0

Reprint 2014

The views and opinions expressed in this book are the contributors' own. They are solely responsible for the facts and authenticity of the sources used in this work. The publisher in no way is liable for the same.

Printed by Vikas® Publishing House Pvt. Ltd

Acknowledgement

We acknowledge the valuable contribution of Seema Sharma, Manager (Publication & Web Marketing), IISSM and thank her for the research and selection of articles and papers for this book from various papers presented in the seminars, workshops and from short-term training courses of IISSM.

We thank Ratna Sinha, Joint Secretary, IISSM for monitoring this project on a day-to-day basis.

We also acknowledge with thanks the support and cooperation of Lt Gen (Retd) Prem Sagar, Director General, IISSM, Brig (Retd) A K Pathak, Director, (Courses) & Col Alok Akhauri, Director (Courses) in making this project a success.

Editor & Executive Chairman, IISSM

Content

Foreword

The Hotel sector in India is one of the fastest growing industries with annual growth rate of 8.8 %. It is worth US $ 17 billion, that is equivalent to approximately Rs 91,800 crore at the September 2012 exchange rate. To safeguard and to keep the hotel industry secured from any external or internal threat, it needs special attention. Writers whose articles appear in this book Hotel Security and Executive Protection have given accounts and analysed the subject that may help in providing protection to executives staying in hotels. The guests, at times, include visiting Heads of States, Presidents, Prime Ministers and Monarchs besides senior executives and corporate honchos from business and industry. The book also deals with protecting hotels from accidents and terrorist attacks.

"The task of executive protection has become increasingly challenging and demanding day by day. The operatives make use of the latest technology and have developed worldwide ramifications through the nexus of terrorists, smugglers and gun runners. Their modus operandi is not sophisticated but has acquired deftness, dexterity and speed. Therefore, this challenge now calls for specialization with a high degree of professionalism." This is what I observe in my opening article.

There are examples of how lives could have been saved with extra precautions and preventive measures taken in time, whether it was the case of the assassination of Prime Minister Indira Gandhi in 1984, or the case of assassination of Georges Besse, President of the Renault car company in 1986.

"The rifle, which killed President Kennedy in 1963, was not more fatal than the knife, which stabbed Caesar. Those who support this view would do well to study the case of General Charles de Gaulle, who, during his term of office as the French president, was the subject of 30 known assassination attempts, all of which failed. President de Gaulle was a difficult person to protect as he often refused to take even elementary precautions and did away with many of the measures likely to save his life. No doubt he enjoyed more than a little good luck during his term of office but he also enjoyed the services of an effective protection-organization", writes B N Prasad in his article Executive Protection. Fire is another major cause of concern for the hotel industry. P Purukayastha writes, "In recent times all over the world, several serious fire accidents have occurred in hotels, resulting in large-scale loss of life and property. As a result of this, the hotel industry has been affected and many tourists intending to holiday prefer to choose motels and other such small establishments, with a view to avoid experiences of holocaust of hotel fires which have been witnessed in many places, world over".

Charlie R A Pierce, an expert in security, talks about the use of CCTV in preventing attacks and or accidents. He says, "Education is an ongoing process of feeding the mind information, sorting that information and then applying it in a productive manner. It should never be the endeavour of an individual to memorize everything about anything. It should instead be the goal of all professionals to learn how and where to find, quickly, the answers and information needed".

I hope you find the book useful and informative.

Ravindra Singh

Editor & Executive Chairman, IISSM

Contributors

R K Sinha, Chairman & Managing Director, SIS (India) Limited

As a writer/journalist. Ravindra Kishore Sinha is a known face. After having a long stint in journalism, he ventured into enterprise and established SIS (India) Limited of which he is now the Chairman and Managing Director. Despite being involved full time as a corporate head in his enterprise, he finds time to scribble and occasionally writes. On the subject of security, he is a prolific speaker and writer.

B N Prasad, IPS

B N Prasad, an Indian Police Service officer, retired as the Inspector General of CRPF.

Anthony Foran, CPP

He is a Certified Protection Professional, Security Management at ASIS International. During his 12 year long experience in the field of security, he has faced so many security challenges that it has made him a Security Expert. From 2001 to 2006, he was the Security Manager at Taj Residency, Bangalore, where he formulated and implemented the hotel's security strategy in line with the group's mission and vision.

With his comprehensive knowledge of global security strategy, procedure, policies and technology, he worked at Dell International Services, Indìa Private Limited, Bangalore till 2009 as Security Manager. In 2010 he joined Paladin Security, Mississauga, Ontario, Canada as Security Officer.

Prof (Dr) Proloy Purkayastha

Dr. P Purkayastha has done B Sc (H), B, Ch (Engg), M Sc (Engg - IE & OR) [UK], PhD, MBIMLondon], MORSI. MICh E,and has 24 years of experience in mMultinational and GOI undertakings. Since 1975, he has been associated with the Calcutta University, the Jadavpur University, IGNOU and BITS, Pillani and BE College (Deemed University).

His area of interest is Operation Management, Material Management, Technology Management, DSS, Project Management, Public System Management, Logistic Management and related research. Hntlye is at present Professor and Dean of the Indian Institute of Social Welfare and Business Management, Kolkata.

Charlie R A Pierce

Charlie R A Pierce, president of IPC Technologies, Inc., has 35 years experience in the security industry and is considered a leading authority on the design and application of CCTV and integrated security solutions. He is the author of The Professional's Guide to CCTV—considered by many to be the bible of the CCTV industry.

Protecting High-Profile People

R K Sinha

Introduction

The task of executive protection has become increasingly challenging and demanding day by day. The operatives make use of the latest technology and have developed worldwide ramifications through the nexus of terrorists, smugglers and gun runners. Their modus operandi is not sophisticated but has acquired deftness, dexterity and speed. Therefore, this challenge now calls for specialization with a high degree of professionalism.

Thousands of senior executives of large number of corporations throughout the world are vulnerable to the threat and need executive protection. Similar is the plight of thousands of other high profile personalities, who have achieved excellence in their respective fields like arts and culture, music, sports, theatre, cinema, journalism or politics. Various terrorists and criminal groups know it very well due to their ant position in the society.

Kidnapping of these executives and high profile personalities can fetch criminals or terrorists handsome ransom money, wide media coverage, and also perhaps a jail term. Terrorists indulge in these activities to create panic and to undermine the confidence of the people in the establishment.

The Threat

The threats which a normal high profile executive faces today are:

1. Threat of physical assault or humiliation at work place by a violent mob of workers,
2. Threat of mental torture to self and family through anonymous calls and letters,
3. Threat of mugging while moving on the streets,
4. Threat of kidnapping and abduction for ransom or for blackmailing, and
5. Threat of assassination.

An important point to note, when we discuss about threat potential, is that all the possibilities of the threats mentioned above, also apply to the family members of the executives. Another interesting point to note is that as we raise the protection level of an executive, the probability of the family members becoming soft target rises. The reason being that the moment a targeted executive becomes a difficult target, due to increased level of protection, the attention is automatically shifted to the family members, who are likely to be less protected.

Reason for Increasing Threat

A number of reasons may be attributed to the increasing threat perception of the executives during the past few years. Some of the important reasons are:

(a) Increasing Expectation,

(b) Diminishing Loyalties,
(c) General lawlessness,
(d) Unemployment,
(e) Terrorism,
(f) Irresponsible trade unionism or political movements/disaffected employees,
(g) Unethicalcompetitions,
(h) Disproportionate reasons, and
(i) Ineffective law enforcement.

Threatened Executive

People ask me how to identify a threatened executive and the answer lies in the following words: "Any executive who is required to take such decisions on behalf of the country which may subsequently benefit or harm an individual or a group of people, whether workers or outsiders, is a potentially threatened executive."However this is a general statement and this definition may vary according to changing situations. Therefore in executive protection, maximum weightage should be given by any protective agency to the identification of the threatened executive, the level of threat perception, and the persons/groups from whom the threat is anticipated.

Vulnerability

There are a number of vulnerable points in executive protection and a number of situations when even highly protected executives might become vulnerable or a soft target. The following few points are important to note:

(a) Casualness at home and office,
(b) Drive between home and office,
(c) Check-points and bottlenecks,
(d) Travelling executives,
(e) School-going children,

(f) Housewives when alone at home or while shopping, and

(g) Children in playground.

Case Studies

There are a number of interesting case studies from which we can draw lessons. However, I would like to discuss the following ten case studies involving five businessmen, threepolitical leaders, and two diplomats:

1. Assassination of German businessman, Alfred Herrhausen on 30 November1989.
2. Assassination of Georges Besse, President of Renault carcompany, on 17 November, 1986.
3. Assassination of two former prime ministers of India,. Indira Gandhi and Rajiv Gandhi, and former Lankan President. R Premadasa.
4. Assassination of Telco Executive, S N Sahay and kidnapping of another TELCO executive, one Mr Pande.
5. Assassination of a tea garden owner,Surinder Paul.
6. Kidnapping and release of a Ranchi business executive, R S Harlalka.
7. Kidnapping and release of Mukesh Jain of Pasupati Acrylon, New Delhi.

Now let us discuss these case studies in brief to draw lessons from them:

ALFRED HERRHAUSEN: A renowned, multi-billionaire, German businessman. Alfred Herrhausen was killed on the way from his home to the office on 30 November 1989.

It is important to note thatHerrhausen was fully aware of the threat and had already taken possible precautions for his own protection and for the protection of his family. A custom-built armoured car was manufactured specially for the movement of. Herrhausen. It cost a few million US dollars. Best available commandos were deployed for the protection ofHerrhausen and his family. WhenHerrhausen went out of his house, a pilot car moved ahead of his car and an escort car followed. In all the three vehicles, trained commandos with sophisticated weapons were positioned.

In spite of high-level protection,Herrhausen was killed just 300 yards away from his home while he was driving to his office. Now, let us see how it happened.

Herrhausen lived in a very rich neighbourhood and there was absolutely no scope of mounting any surveillance of his house or his movement. Therefore, the terrorist put one of its members under cover of a one-man crew for road repairs six weeks in advance i.e. exactly on 18th October, 1989. This single-member repair troop kept on repairing the road around the house ofHerrhausen for almost six weeks till he was able to blow his car to pieces. The modus operandi of the entire operation was highly sophisticated and well planned. There was a children's park about 300 yards away fromHerrhausen's house which was a checkpoint.Herrhausen had to come to that point, for taking the main road leading out of his residential colony. Now, onthe same day when the single -roop repair team arrived i.e. on 18 October 1989, a very expensive children's-bicycle was thrown in the park, very close to the side of the road. Naturally, it attracted attention of the other children and even some passersby. They inspected the bicycle and found in its rack sack some video games, comics and toys, all crazy stuff which some child of a rich parent would like to possess. Those who inspected the rack sack laughed and ignored it, treating it as an act of some "crazy boy". The bicycle remained there for a few days and suddenly disappeared from the scene. Those who found the cycle gone,laughed. A couple of days later, the bicycle was again found, thrown at the same place. This time people ignored it. Between 18 October, 1989 and 30 November 1989, the bicycle was thrown and removed from that spot 8 to 10 times, till the people started completely ignoring it and the thrown bicycle had by that time registered in everybody's mind "as a part of the environment of that spot"....

On the morning of 30 November, whenHerrhausen took the turn at that point, his car was blown up by using a high-powered explosive. The terrorist had connected the explosives in the rack sack with the detonating device through a photoelectric beam switch, which was operated through a remote control. As the pilot car ofHerrhausen passed the spot and the car in whichHerrhausen was sitting approached spot, the single man crew operated the switch and established the contact between the remote and the photoelectric cell placed in the rack sack. As. Herrhausen's car crossed the invisible beam the contact was broken and it detonated the explosive, blowingHerrhausen's vehicle to pieces.

Lessons: An in-depth analysis of this case brings out the following lapses:

(a) AlthoughHerrhausen's level of protection was adequate, the intelligence feedback was either not there or it was nonexistent

(b) No one in the neighbourhood, including the guards in the house ofHerrhausen tried to check the bonafide of the single man crew, especially when he was taking more time than was required for the job, and was working long hours, even without the visit of any supervisors for inspection during the six-week period. No one even bothered to check with the city administration whether the repair was authorized by them.

(c) They all laughed at the abandoned bicycle. It did not arouse anybody's suspicion,even when a stand for parking children's bicycles was at hand and yet a cycle was thrown and removed a number of times from the same site,only to make it acceptable as a part of the environment.

GEORGES BESSE: the president of Renault car companyGeorges Besse was killed in his portico while he was about to get into the car in the morning of 17 November 1986. Georges Besse had a very routine life. On the evening of 17 November1986, whenBesse emerged from his chauffeur-driven car, a terrorist couple rode up to him on a motorcycle and shot him from a point blank range.

The terrorist group named Action Directe took responsibility for this killing. Almost five months later, during March 1987, a hideout of Action Directe" was raided by the French police. As many as sixty well–edited video cassettes were recovered. One of them was on the lifestyle and movement pattern ofGeorges Besse. Another cassette was related to a French General, who had also been killed by Action Directe. However, 58 precious lives were saved due to the recovery of these video cassettes.

Lessons: Lessons drawn from this Assassination:

(a) Terrorist groups do make a very close observation of the lifestyle of the target. Therefore, if the intelligence network of the corporation/individual is efficient, they can detect and blow off the surveillance mounted by the terrorist.

(b) A threatened executive should not stick to a routine.

(c) Home, which a person considers as the safest place, is one of the most vulnerable places from the point of view of executive protection.

INDIRA GANDHI: Prime Minister Indira Gandhi's murder is a well-known case and does not require any detailed description. Gandhi was killed by her own guard within the premises of her residence.

Lessons: I would only like to discuss the important lessons from this case:

(a) Indira Gandhi was advised by the Intelligence Bureaunot to keepmembers of a certain religious community on her personal protection staff as they were disaffected. Mrs Gandhi disregarded this advice as she felt that it would not be consistent with her ideal of secularism. The lesson drawn from this is that disregarding the advice of the security agency might lead to disaster.

(b) It has been established during investigation that there was distinct changes in thelifestyle of these guards for a couple of months before the assassination. For example, they used to move about in hired taxis and did not use the transport provided by the government. They also started eating out more frequently, a few weeks before the assassination. The assassins and their collaborators were meeting regularly at secret hideouts and visiting places of their worships to renew their oath to kill Mrs Gandhi.The obvious lesson drawn is that there should be intensive surveillance on the personnel security staff and body guards of the executives and to be more specific, any change in their lifestyle, spending-pattern and associates must be taken notice of.

(c) On the morning of the attack, the two bodyguards had managed to get the places of their assigned duty changed to a vulnerable point on some special plea. As a result, both stationed themselves at the same place and supported each other when they fired at Mrs Gandhi. No security supervisor on duty had taken note of this change in their place of duty.

RAJIV GANDHI: Former Prime Minister of India,Rajiv Gandhi, was killed by members of the terrorist group LTTE (Liberation Tigers of Tamil Elam) while going to address a public meeting on 21 May 1991 at Sriperumbudur in Tamil Nadu. In this case, a female member of a suicide squad of LTTE acted as a human bomb and while garlanding Gandhi, blew herself up killing more than two dozen people including Rajiv Gandhi.

Lessons: Like in the case of Georges Besse, the terrorist group had minutely studied the movement pattern and public meetings of Mr. Gandhi. His politeness and warmth while accepting garlands and flowers, especially from women and children, had been carefully observed and noted by the terrorist group and accordingly the assassination plot was planned and executed.

(a) The tendency of the Congress leader to mingle in the crowd disregarding the well-established security restrictions was also exploited by the suicide squad.

(b) The organizers of the meeting are also to be blamed for not adhering to the prescribed security regulations for admitting party men into the inner cordon.

(c) The commission of enquiry had pinpointed the lapses and inadequacy in the security arrangements for the meeting. It has held that the threat perception of an individual does not diminish after he demits office. In this case, Rajiv Gandhi was not covered by the Special Protection Group when he ceased to be the prime minister. The SPG Act has since been amended to cover former prime ministers and their families for at least five years after they cease to hold the post.

R PREMADASA: Former president of Sri Lanka,R. Premadasa was killed while leading a rally on May Day in 1993.

Lessons:

(a) It is reported that whenPremadasa's rally reached the crossing, there were other small rallies coming from different directions, wanting to merge into the main rally led byPremadasa. The security forces had stopped all other rallies and directed them to followPremadasa's rally.But all other rallies were allowed to merge into his rally to gain popularity; the advice of the security experts were ignored and in the melee, Mr. Premadasa was killed by a member of the suicide squad ofLTTE, again by a human bomb.

(b) It has been learnt that a member of the suicide squad softened some member of the president's personal staff through wine and women and it was he who was the human bomb.

S N SAHAY: In November 1990, S NSahay, dy. general manager of Tata Engineering and Locomotives Co. Ltd was killed at his door step when he stopped his car at the gate of his bungalow and was about to get down to open the main gate.

Lessons: Places near the homes are most vulnerable. The gate of entry should be kept open for the car to speed in without any hindrance. Also the gate must be closed as soon as the car passes through it.

PANDE: A deputy general manager of TELCO, one Mr Pande, was kidnapped while he was attending a meeting in his office. However, due to prompt action of the TELCO security personnel and the police, he was rescued within a few hours and his life could be saved.

Lesson: Work place is equally vulnerable for threatened executives.

SURINDER PAUL: Surinder Paul, a renowned tea garden owner, and brother of the noted industrialist, Swaraj Paul, was assassinated while visiting his tea garden in Assam which isinsurgency affected. He was assassinated at a bottleneck point which was an unavoidable part of his route.

Lesson: Bottleneck points are very vulnerable and it is advised that a pilot car should move ahead to clear bottleneck check points.

R S HARLALKA: R S Harlalka, a senior executive of Ranchi based Usha Martin Industries Ltd was kidnapped while travelling between his house and his office. He was released after several days. It is understood that a handsome amount of ransom was paid for securing his release.

Lesson: The distance between house and office is vulnerable stretch and alertness and precautions are needed, as it is an easy task to find out routine movements like travelling between house and office. Routes and timings should be changed regularly.

MUKESH JAIN: Mukesh Jain, managing director of Pasupati Acrylon Ltd was kidnapped (March 1993) while he was getting out ofhis car after returning home from office. It is reported that he was kidnapped by some terrorist group of Punjab. It is also reported that he was kidnapped by some terrorists who followed his car as it went out of his office. AsJain's car approached his house, the security guard opened the gate and the terrorist-car also entered the house without any resistance. AsJain was getting out of the car he was abducted and whisked away. The security guard who tried to resist was killed on the spot.Jain was released after two weeks. He was held in forests and was moved thousands of miles in a truck. It is reported that a huge ransom was paid to secure his release.

Lessons: Drivers must be trained to watch out for suspicious movements on the way and car followers. Preferably, the threatened executive should himself drive so that he can see the car's rear-view mirror and look out for vehicles following or overtaking his/her vehicle

Critical Areas: The critical threat areas are near home and office and the distancebetween home and office. Few examples:

(a) A German businessman was killed 300 yards away from his home.

(b) A French businessman was assassinated at his door step.

(c) A senior executive of TELCO, at Jamshedpur, was killed in front of his house.

(d) Another senior executive ofTELCO was kidnapped at his work place.

(e) A U.S. military officer was killed 300 yards away from hishome

(f) A Colombian businessman was kidnapped at a distance of 200 yards from his office.

(g) A Romanian diplomat was kidnapped between his home and office.

(h) An Indian businessman was abducted while getting down from his car, from his own portico.

(i) Mrs Gandhi was assassinated at her residence.

(j) **An Indian diplomat kidnapped outside his residence.**

Precautions and Alertness: An executive cannot be protected by the security forces, if he himself is not aware of the threats and does not co-operate fully with the protective agencies.

Observations: Observation is an important aspect in executive protection. It is the responsibility of the security expert to ensure that the executives are trained to observe things like:

(a) Watch out for disaffected employees,
(b) Watch out for abnormal movement near office / home,
(c) Train family members to discuss abnormal incidents,
(d) De-brief children periodically,
(e) Establish identity of visitors, and
(f) Do not hesitate to take protective agencies into confidence.

Counter-Measures: There are numerous counter-measures in the area of executive protection. However, some of the points which every security officer must keep in mind are:

(a) Periodical review of threat perception,
(b) Evaluation of threat level,
(c) Notify concerned executives to observe,
(d) Train executives to observe,
(e) Train Personal Security Officers to protect and not to fight,
(f) Discourage arming of PSOs, and
(g) Strengthen intelligence networks.

Dos and Don'ts: No exercise of executive protection can be successful, if the executives themselves do not adhere to the norms. Therefore, the executives must be trained and advised to follow the minimum norms. Some of the Dos and Don'ts are mentioned below:

Dos: Executives are advised to follow the instructions as far as possible:

1. Evaluate and recognize security threats to self and family periodically as a matter of routine.
2. Trust your security manager / consultant and follow his advice religiously.
3. Take your family and children into confidence about the possible security threats.
4. Train children to observe the surroundings; de-brief them regularly, and discuss a few recent case studies with them in a manner by whichthey become more cautious and better educated and are not scared.
5. Brief children and female members to be alert while playing, shopping.
6. Maintain records of visitors and telephone calls received at your home and office. This record will be a vital document for the investigators in case of any unfortunate event.
7. Train personnel staff, family members and servants to converse briefly on telephone and divulge no specific information about your travel plans or movements.
8. Train your driver to identify any change in environment and to react quickly. Tell him what to look for.
9. Keep the doors locked while driving. Never give any lift on the way. Do not stop to help victims of an accident as it might be an ambush. Instead, inform the nearest police station.
10. Train driver and self in routine vehicle inspection before starting the vehicle; inspect break-pipes, rod ends, oil, water, tyres, locks, undercarriage, luggage boot, battery etc.
11. Keep on changing route and timing of driving to the work place. Watch out for any vehicle following, possible ambushes on the way, usual signs like traffic-jams on highways, deserted roads etc. Be careful at bottlenecks and check points.
12. Maintain a low profile while travelling.
13. Search thoroughly and look for suspicious objects while

checking into hotel rooms; ensure that the lock and key are working properly.

14. Keep in touch with family and office on a daily basis while on tour.
15. Keep a watch on activities of disaffected employees / contractors/ ex-employees with grouse etc. They can be potential trouble makers.
16. Remain calm and cool in case of emergency.

Don'ts: Executives are advised to avoid the following:

1. Never take security casually. Maximum lives have been lost due to this kind of approach only.
2. Don't hesitate to take your security expert into confidence. Never ignore advice of your security expert.
3. Don't ignore an anonymous letter, or call, or caution signals given by family members and friends. Every feedback is important for executive protection.
4. Don't meet any unknown visitor at office or entertain any stranger at home, directly and without screening the guests.
5. Do not encourage casual and informal talks on servants or family members unless the caller is very well known.
6. Avoid divulging information about travel plans, movements, etc. on telephone.
7. Do not take into confidence even your driver or personal staff about timings and routes in advance.
8. Never be ignorant of the surroundings whether driving self or riding a chauffeur- driven car.
9. Avoid things which might fully involve you while driving, like listening to your favourite music on high volume, reading a newspaper, magazine or serious discussions with co- travellers.
10. Avoid publicizing the programme of travel. Your travel plan should only be known to the people who need to know it.

11. Do not make friends with strangers while driving / travelling/ flying, or when in a new city.
12. Never visit localities which are not very well known, while on tour avoid sidewalks and dark lanes.
13. Do not carry heavy cash while travelling.
14. Avoid keeping valuables in hotel room.
15. Do not panic in case of any emergency.
16. Do not try to resist or react violently while in hostage situation.

***

Protecting The Most Protected

B N Prasad

The problem of providing protection to the executives from assassinations, kidnapping or some lesser form of injury is a long-standing one. It has become more complex and difficult because of the revolution in the means of transport, modes of communication and sophisticated weapons. The rifle, which killed President Kennedy in 1963, was not more fatal than the knife, which stabbed Caesar. Those who support this view would do well to study the case of General de Gaulle, who during his term of office as the French president, was the subject of 30 known assassination attempts, all of which failed. President de Gaulle was a difficult person to protect as he often refused to take even elementary precautions and did away with many of the measures likely to save his life. No doubt he enjoyed more than a little good luck during his term of office but he also enjoyed the services of an effective protection-organization.

An examination of successful assassinations in recent times will almost invariably reveal avoidable weaknesses in security. Often the weakness is in the security system, or the lack of any system. Often it displays a lack of knowledge and training on the part of those responsible for security and usually it also displays a simple human failure. President Lincoln was assassinated because his bodyguard went for a drink leaving him unguarded for a short time. Lee Harvey Oswald, who assassinated President Kennedy, was under investigation by the FBI, but those responsible for guarding the president, were not notified of his activities. In February 1972 Ulster Unionist MP John Taylor was shot as he walked to his car. His protecting officer was too far away to take effective action and there is every reason to believe that the location of that officer was very significant. There are number of cases which indicate that the position of the protecting officer is very crucial. No matter systems evolve, there will always be failure. In the final analysis, a system depends on human beings, and human beings will fail occasionally. Despite this, if the problem is properly understood and if proper strategies and tactics are developed; it is possible to provide a very high degree of protection to executives/public figures.

The Problem

The Warren Commission Report contains some useful information about certain aspects of the organization system of a protection service. A study of the problem should establish:

(a) The type of person likely to be given protection,
(b) The nature of the activity and the location in which the subject might be found,
(c) The method of attack likely to be used, and
(d) The type of person/organization likely to be involved in the attack.

From the study of these factors, it should be possible to develop an effective protection strategy and then to produce tactics suitable for various situations under which an attack might take place.

The Subject

Protection against assassination, kidnapping or other attacks may be provided to a wide range of people and the nature of the problem will vary according to the office or position of the subject. Six categories might be considered:-

(a) The head of the state of the country

(b) Domestic politicians of very senior rank such as prime minister, chief minister, etc.

(c) Foreign head of states, senior politicians or diplomats to whom the level of threats are considerably high.

(d) Junior politicians whose posts are very sensitive.

(e) Senior officials such as judges, prosecutors, and occasionally, senior police or army officers dealing with specific problems.

(f) In special cases, it might be necessary to protect private citizens.

Subject Activity

The possible activities of a person subject to police protection are limitless, but specific problems might be considered when the potential target is

(a) Within a private residence or other building to which only identifiable persons have access.

(b) In a hotel or other building where large number of people have access to areas close to the subject

(c) Travelling by car on a road journey.

(d) Travelling by trains, plane or a boat.

(e) Working in crowded areas, possibly electioneering or meeting people.

(f) Travelling in a formal procession.

(g) Speaking at public meetings or other large gatherings either in the open or in a building.

(h) Performing some public ceremony such as laying wreath or opening a building.

Method of Attack

A very careful examination of attacks on executive/public figures indicates that it is possible to categorize them according to the nature of the attack and that, apart from exceptions, the method of attack will identify the type of attacker. Six methods might be considered:

(I) Close-Quarters Attack: The close quarter attack is usually made with a pistol but knife and other weapons may also feature. The following examples will typify this close quarter attack:

(a) In July 1986, the leader of the Australian parliamentary opposition had just got into his car after making a speech, when 8 youths ran towards the car and fired at him. The attacker's explanation was that he felt he was nobody and would remain nobody unless he did something out of the ordinary.

(b) In September 1901, the last man in a line of people waiting to meet President McKinley of the USA had a handkerchief around his hand concealing a pistol. When the president came close to the man, he shot him through the body. The attacker said he thought the president was energy of the people.

(c) In December 1972, a mentally deranged man was waiting in a line of people who were to greet the wife of the President of the Philippines. Suddenly, the man rushed forward and stabbed her with a long knife. His motive was not clear. The same method of attack had been used against the Pope when he had visited Philippines.

(d) In November 1972, a woman posing as a journalist waited for the British prime minister to arrive at Egmont Palace, Brussels, when he arrived she threw a tin of black ink on himfrom touching distance. Her reasons were concerned with the plans for the development of an area of London. Such incidents may be thought to be quite trivial but its consequences could well have been fatal.

(e) Mahatma Gandhi used to attend a prayer meeting in the evening which was known to all. On 30 January 1948 while he was going to attend the prayer meeting, an unidentified person, later on whose name was disclosed as Nathuram Godse approached him and opened fire at him with a revolver from a close range. Mahatma Gandhi was killed on the spot. Nathuram Godse was immediately caught and held by the public and was sentenced to death after regular trial.

(f) On 31 October 1984 a very unfortunate incident took place in which the security guard who provided protection to Prime Minister of India, Indira Gandhi, fired at her and killed her on the spot. This incident is an eye-opener, in future while deploying guards for providing security to the VIPs, antecedents as well as the records of those guards must also be scrutinized before they are deployed. The security guards should also be changed after every 3 months and the guards should not be allowed to go on leave during their tenure of posting. In this case the guard who killed Indira Gandhi had returned from leave and it is suspected that he was influenced by some militants.

(g) In Bihar, when Bhagwat Jha Azad, the then Chief Minister of Bihar, visited an area to visit the place of massacre in a village in Jehanabad, a person standing close to him blackened his face. This could have been a serious offence had the attacker hurt Azad with a weapon.

(h) Prime Minister Rajiv Gandhi was killed by a bomb blast while he was being garlanded. Had the proper security arrangements ofnot allowing anyone to approach the VIP, been strictly followed, the attack could have been avoided. But since instructions were not strictly followed, it was easier for the attackers to approach Rajiv Gandhi without being properly checked.

(i) In an attack of the type mentioned above, there is a very high probability of the arrest of the attacker, and in many cases the attackers seem to be seeking arrest and subsequent trial. Despite this, such attackers do not display a death-wish or suggest a desire to perish with their victims. They usually feel that they are serving a cause and wish to be seen as heroes of that cause.

(II) Mid-Range Attack

An attack from a mid-range is most likely to involve rapid fire weapons such as machine guns, but may also involve pistols or rifles, mostly used by terrorists, as is being done in the valley of Jammu and Kashmir. Here I would also like to mention that L N Mishra, former railway minister, while addressing a meeting at the railway station of Samastipur on 2 January 1975 was injured seriously by the bursting of a bomb placed on the dais. He died subsequently. In this particular incident I was present as the DIG. of Darbhanga Range and was badly injured along with the railway minister. Since no proper information about the possibility of an attack was given, no attention could be paid towards the activities of some disgruntled elements not happy with lL N Mishra. In this case all preventive actions were taken as per the Blue Book, but as there was some slackness in allowing the public to come very near to the dais, the bad elements had the advantage of keeping the bomb on the dais which exploded and not only injured Mishra, but also many other persons who were there, including myself.

(III) Long-Range Snapper Attack

This method has attracted a disproportionate amount of attention because of the assassination of President Kennedy in November 1963 when a man using a rifle fitted with a telescopic site fired from a building overlooking the route at the range of 190' In fact, this method of assassination is rare.

The problem of providing protection is frequently seen in terms of the duties of the close protection officer, the bodyguard. A myth created around this figure produces an image of a man who will spot an assassin before he makes his attack, and will then foil and attack singlehandedly by fast shooting or some other physical action. The close protection officers have an important part to play in providing protection, no doubt, but a proper examination of the available evidence will show that the task demands a great deal more than providing tough, fit, well-trained bodyguards. Shooting by a close protection officer has rarely, if ever, saved the life of a subject. There can be no doubt that the best way to protect someone is to keep him away from danger as threat arises. The August 1966 attack on de Gaulle was foiled not by engaging in a gun battle but skillful driving of the car which took him out of a danger area. The attack on Princess Anne in 1974 was intended to kidnap her. If the attacker had meant to kill he would most certainly have succeeded. Well if the royal car had simply accelerated, there would have been little or no danger to the Princess. The close protection officer is the person of last report who comes into play when other more effective measures have failed. His role is a small part of the protection operation, and it is by no means the most important part. The provision of an effective protection service is a long term problem and like other long-term problems of a complex nature, it requires the development and maintenance of suitable strategy, the application of appropriate tactics and thorough training at both command and junior level.

Strategy

An effective long-term strategy for protection duties involves four important steps applicable to all complex operations:

1. Intelligence
2. Prevention
3. Reaction
4. Follow up

Each of these measures is vital and a failure of any of them could significantly affect the public figure concerned.

Subject

Details about the subject must be furnished by the intelligence wing and on the basis of that information, necessary protection can be provided.

Attacker

The identification of persons likely to be involved in attacks will often help to indicate both the subject and the probable method of attack. The recognition of dangerous extremist-groups or of specific individuals within such groups is likely to be facilitated by informants, agents and surveillance. It must also be recognized that extremist-groups do not usually reach a dangerous stage overnight. Before such an organization reaches a stage where it might embark on assassination or kidnappings, usually there will have been a phase during which it would have issued its demands, its threats, and its ultimatum. A careful check on the propaganda outburst of a newly-formed organization will often indicate a need for closer surveillance. With organizations identified as threats, the activities in this field are often carried out by the younger, less stable elements. The identification of these individuals is most likely to be by means of information or surveillance. In many countries there are likely to be many unstable people but only a very small number of them could be dangerous in this field. The task of isolating information about these individuals requires a widely based organization, operating continuously in sifting information supplied from the local police or from specialist units. A good deal of research has been done on the problem, particularly in USA.

The Timing

Details of the timing of a particular attack might be supplied by informants, by agents or through surveillance and an intelligence-organization must be geared up to obtain and use such direct information. Good intelligence should however, do a great deal more than that.

The Method

The final task of intelligence is to indicate where and how attack might be made. The forecasting of the method of attack is of course an uncertain business, yet it is clear that a great deal can be done. Any detailed study of assassinations and other attacks shows a remarkable amount of copying. It is well known that terrorist groups are now linked internationally, and that they exchange ideas, personnel and weapons. The unstable attacker has been identified and a major risk that he takes, is often copying a recent attack method. Numerous examples exist where good intelligence might have alerted those responsible to the type of threat likely to exist. The attack on the Australian opposition leader in 1966 was followed four months later by an attack on the Australian prime minister using exactly the same type of weapon and the same method. The attack on Imelda Marcos in 1972 was a carbon-copy of an attack on the Pope when he visited Philippines, a short time before. This phenomenon of copying is well known in most areas of crime.

Good intelligence, as a means of forestalling an assassination, is the best possible protection to any subject. Even where it can't entirely prevent an attack, it might at least alert officers on the ground to specify dangers and so enable them to prevent the attack.

Prevention

Whilst recognizing that intelligence is invaluable, it cannot be expected to be infallible. The measures most likely to provide adequate protectionsare those designed to prevent a planned attack which has not been discovered by intelligence. Prevention may be achieved in two ways

(i) Unpredictability in certain circumstances; it is be possible to make the movement of the subject so unpredictable that attackers are not be able to plan or prepare on attack. This might involve route-planning and route-changing.,

(ii) Preliminary check–when a route or location is fixed either by choice or by force of circumstances, measures should be taken to check the route or the location prior to the arrival of the subject with a view to discover and remove any would-be attacker, bombs or other devices before the subject comes into contact with them.

Unpredicability

The planning and varying of routes, frequent and unpredictable changes of routine and similar measures are designed to make it difficult for the attacker to prepare. The predictabilities of the lives and routines of many subjects impose severe limitations on these measures. Public figures such as head of the state or politicians must, in many cases, adhere to prearranged and widely publicized routes and schedules, yet many routines, journeys and visits do not create such a requirement and many terrorist attacks have succeeded because of unnecessary predictability. Where a routine, non-public journey is to be made, the ideal method may be to survey a number of possible commanders or the subject himself selects one at random. Ideally, it should be possible to change the route mid-way through a journey. Any terrorist attack is likely to be preceded by a period of watching, studying the various routes and seeking entire routes, the attacker may well have time to make their preparation.

Whatever variations are made to the routes, the origin of destination is likely to be known and so the route will be predictably close to each. Preventive measures of the second type should be taken. In many cases, there will be justification for using decoy vehicles and personnel having one vehicle leave openly, whilst the subject takes a less open and possibly indirect route.

Over a period of time, this process of route and routine variation becomes inconvenient to the subject and to the protecting officer as it involves a great deal of detailed planning and effort. Admiral Carrero Blanco, the prime minister of Spain was blown off by his attackers because the route was known to them.

Preliminary Attack

The route or location of the subject may be fixed and publicly known well in advance. A study of assassination shows that attackers will frequently wait in position for a considerable time and there are number of cases where it can be shown that police activity in advance of the subject has prevented an attack. Officers, who are familiar with the physical layout of the area should be deployed as identifier of suspects, ahead of the subject so that they might intercept an attacker before the subject arrives. The searching of the route or a building or in checking of people arriving at a function such as public meeting may seem like an impossible task, but the responsive identification process described will play a very important part and will greatly increase a chance of success. Where an intelligence unit has created for itself reputation for efficiency, its success will add to the uncertainty in the criminal's mind. He will never know just how much information the police have about him and his intention, and he may disclose himself or at least give up his attempt in the face of police activity. In addition to looking at people, the preliminary checks should involve an examination of the physical features of the route or building. If the officers concerned are not sufficiently familiar with the area they should check the route or building well in advance and check it again shortly before subject is due. They may then note any suspicious changes or preparation. A pile of sand at the road side hid a bomb designed to blow up General de Gaulle. A newly painted line on a building, painted by a workman who was not working could have betrayed the Booby Trap set for

Admiral Carrero Blanco. This preliminary checking for suspects and other signs can and do pay dividends. In the buildings, stopping places, danger points along a road, and other identified areas of theft must be searched in advance of the arrival of the subject and must then be secured so that no bomb can be planted after the search. The effectiveness of preliminary checks must be done of the press reporters and the photographers because it has been seen that on many occasions photographers have taken advantages of their position and betrayed the security arrangement. Photographers however, sometimes help also in taking the photographs of the culprits and sometimes these photographing have been found useful in locating the criminals.

Where a non-specified route can be selected at short notice, the use of preliminary check will depend on the circumstances and on a realistic, but cautious assessment of the threats. It might be decided to check each of several routes and to maintain surveillance on all of them until the subject has gone.

The subject of preventive measure is to ensure that the assassins or their weapons areprevented from coming into contact with the subject either by making the subject movement unpredictable or by identifying potential attackesr or theirpreparation before the subject reaches them. Such preventive measures have worked on many occasions and there must be many more cases where an unsuspected would-be attacker has been deterred.

When intelligence and prevention fail, the police must provide the greatest degree of physical protection in the circumstances. Public figures will generally demand the lowest possible level of obvious activity and will not accept a degree of protection which would isolate them. Physical protection must take account of the types of attack and of the measure most likely to frustrate such attack.

It will be necessary to have at least two officers concerned with close protection. One to concentrate solely on getting the subject cleared and another to repel the attacker or otherwise facilitate his removal. It is impossible to provide reasonable degree of protection with a single body guard no matter who he might be. Only when the subject is clear of the area of possible danger should a secondary operation be started to deal with the attacker. Where for some reasons it is not possible to get the subject cleared, contingency plan will cater for action to protect him at the point of attack. This basic protective action must continue if the attacker is known to be killed or arrested. The subject must be removed from the area until it is clear that there are no sources of danger and that any crowds are completely under control. If the subject is travelling by car, the car subject at once should be driven off as far as practicable to some prearranged place. This may mean diverting form the fixed route and in the case of a lengthy journey it will be necessary to select a number of safe places along the route. The driver's familiarity with the area should be such that he can take any one of a number of different routes to anyone of the safe places. If the subject is walking through crowded place, a safe place should be predecided so that if an attack takes place everyone will know to clear the way. If the subject is addressing a meeting, the safe place should be a bullet resistant lectern provided for the purpose or it might be a room close to the platform in which the subject can be taken quickly.

A study of the problems as mentioned above should establish:

I. The type of person likely to be given protection.

II. The nature of the activity and the location in which the subject might be found.

III. The method of attack likely to be used.

IV. The type of person or organization likely to be involved in the attack.

From a study of these factors, it should be possible to develop an effective protection strategy and then to produce tactics suitable for the various situations under which an attack might take place.

***

Effects of Terrorism

Anthony Foran

Terrorism has many facets. Sometimes the focus is on mode of operation of terrorist organizations and at other times the emphasis is on motivation and characteristics of terror outfits.

In the book "Political Terrorism" Schmidt and Youngman cited 109 different definitions of Terrorism, which they obtained in a survey of leading academics in the field. From the definitions, the authors isolated the following recurring elements in order of their statistical appearance in the definitions. Violent force (appeared in 83.5% of the definition); Political (65%); fear, emphasis on terror (51%); threats (47%); psychological effects and anticipated reactions (41.5%); discrepancy between the targets and the victims (37.5%); intentional, planned systematic organized action (32%); methods of combat, strategy, tactics (30.5%).

Countries of the world also view "Terrorism" from their own

perspective. In India for an act to be considered as "Terrorism" three factors have been stressed: intent "to threaten the unity, integrity, security or sovereignty of India", or "to strike terror in the people" mode, i.e. use of violence such as bombs, fire arms, chemicals etc. or by any other means and the end effect of causing death, injuries, destruction of property, disruption of essential supplies, etc.

The Arab League in the past has made statements saying that "activities aimed at liberation and self determinations are not in the category of terrorism".

Abu Iyad who was one of Yasser Arafat's deputies once stated, "by nature, and even on ideological grounds, I am firmly opposed to political murder and, more generally to terrorism. Nevertheless, unlike many others, I do not confuse revolutionary violence with terrorism, or operations that constitute political acts with others that do not". In other words terrorism and political violence are two different unconnected phenomena and a political motive makes the activity respectable.

Boaz Ganor, director of the International Policy Institute for Counter-Terrorism in Israel, defines terrorism as "... the international use of or threat to use violence against civilians or against civilian targets in order to attain political aims".

The statement "One man's terrorist is another man's freedom fighter" has been not only a cliché but also one of the most difficult obstacles in coping with terrorism.

As you see the struggle to define Terrorism is sometimes as hard as the struggle against terrorism itself. The helplessness of our governments and their respective intelligence agencies to prevent terrorism suggest that this threat to the Hotel Industry will be an extremely difficult one to deal with.

Prior to linking terrorism to the hotel industry, let us first observe the changing faces of terrorism, which is one of the most important issues facing the world today.

From the bombings of the US embassies in Nairobi, Kenya and Tanzania in 1998 to the attack on the World Trade Center and Pentagon in 2001, from the bombing of a tourist resort in Bali in October 2002 to the attack on a Hindu temple in Gujarat, from the hostage taking incident in Moscow by Chechen rebels to what have might been an attack on the shopping centre–Ansal Plaza in Delhi on the eve of Diwali, all of these show there is no stopping this hidden enemy from acting in a number of different ways.

One thing which is fast emerging as a common factor the world over is that terrorist organizations are now opting more for "Scale" and "Civilian Targeting" as means to achieve their ends. The trend is towards higher casualties. Religiously motivated terrorist groups represent a growing hatred towards certain nationalities of the world. Other terrorist groups are driven by visions of a post-apocalyptic future or by ethnic hatred. Such groups may lack any concrete political goal other than to punish their enemies by killing as many of them as possible, seemingly without concern about alienating sympathizers. Increasingly, attacks are less likely to be followed by claims of responsibility or list of political demands.

Terrorism in some parts of the world has already emerged in the midst of daily activities leaving a fear, which is there, and at the same time not there because most believe that "I will not fall prey" to the Terrorist activity. TRUE! But what about the organizations we work in, modes of transport we travel in, the hotel you stay in, the school we send our children to, the shopping centre we shop at? Venues of daily activity like these can be potential targets for terrorist activity. In order to analyse this, first let us discuss the two most common aims of most of the terrorist groups in the world today.

The first and foremost aim is publicity. Most terrorist organizations create publicity in order to draw attention to their cause. This they do by making innocent civilians pay for their publicity bill in blood.

From Black August in 1998 (Omagh Bombing and the attack on the U.S. embassies) to the World Trade Center attack in September 2001 to the bomb attack in Bali in 2002, the media has to rethink about how to report terrorist attacks. Governments, media and public opinion for instance are getting clouded by the usage of the terms like "militants", "insurgents", and "freedom fighters". Yet terrorism thrives, thanks to the political arguments of the terrorist's "cause". That's where the media comes in. The terrorist is wrongly portrayed as a product of society's unwillingness to listen to his problems. The fact is that the terrorist has to be delinked from whatever "cause" he is espousing. No cause justifies his means. The people killed in the bomb attacks in Bali had nothing to do with the fight for an Islamic state in Indonesia or the women and children killed in the attack on the Akshardham temple (September 2002)in Gujarat had nothing to do with the riots or reprisal attacks in Gujarat. Yet innocent lives anywhere anytime in the world are at risk because terrorists know they are the routes to prime time coverage and banner headlines. And that is exactly why the media needs to ask itself: Is it necessary to report the name of terrorist groups claiming responsibility for an attack? Is it necessary to report the demands and manifestoes of terrorist groups reporting them like any other press release? These aren't questions involving the detached professional routine, the responsibility to report the "truth", or bagging a "scoop"; it's a question of a far greater responsibility of not playing into the terrorist's hands. Publicity is the terrorist's objective. So don't give him publicity. Delink him from the "cause" whatever the cause maybe. Otherwise indiscreet media treatment of terrorist attacks obviously encourages terrorism.

The second aim is to create fear and panic and undermine the confidence of society in their respective governments. The terrorist's primary aim is to create fear within the target population, with the intention that this fear is translated into pressure on the government to accede to the terrorist's demands in order to stave off further terror attacks. Modern terrorism has now focused on civilian targets as they are not only easy targets but also effective ones. The randomness of the attacks contributes to the general anxiety. The message is: anyone, anywhere, at any time maybe the target of the next attack. This threat undermines the ability of the civilian population to live a normal life. When every action must involve planning for how to survive a potential attack at a random time and place, the daily routine becomes fraught with anxiety. For example the sniper attacks in Maryland, USA. and the suicide bombings in Israel, they create more of a psychological fear whereas these fears have no connection to reality. The likelihood of being harmed in a terror attack is less than the likelihood of being harmed in a traffic accident or an accident at home or workplace. In fact the chances of dying from a serious illness are far more common than the chances of being even slightly injured in a terror attack. Nonetheless by using psychological manipulation the terrorists succeed in creating disproportionate anxiety in relation to the actual threat–a kind of irrational panic. Thus the physical damage created by terrorism may be statistically less than that of traffic accidents or other mishaps, but the atmosphere created by the terrorist's act cast a greatly magnified shadow over society, far in excess of its statistical risk to individuals.

Terrorism also aims at trying to destabilize the government directly. Take the case of the bombings in Bali. Indonesia was an affordable tourist destination for forcigners. However the bombings have effectively destroyed one of the country's key industries. It has definitely caused a serious setback to the government and may set the stage to a social and political turmoil. In short, the people who set off the bomb knew exactly what they were doing. They have also succeeded in undermining the world's opinion on the government of Indonesia. It has also resulted in issuing of fresh travel warnings for the entire South-East Asia.

The activities they are engaged in, in order to achieve their aims are:

1. **Bombings**–Latest being the Bali bombings by the Jemaah Islamiah, which killed 181 people.
2. **Hostage situations**–The largest hostage incident in the world was the one in which around 700 people were taken hostage by forty armed Chechen terrorists at a theatre in Moscow on 23 October, 2002. Another was an incident in May 2002 in which a lone Chechen gunman burst into a 5-star hotel in Istanbul and took thirteen hostages.
3. **Assassinations**–The shooting of an Israeli cabinet minister at the door of his hotel, Hyatt Regency in East Jerusalem.
4. **Biological and Chemical weapons**–The 1995 release of a chemical agent in a Tokyo subway by the Aum Shinrikyo groups.
5. Nuclear Threats (Weapons of Mass Destruction-WMDs)

These terrorist organizations are so effective in carrying out the above because of the following reasons:

1. Extension of the Terrorist's Geographic Reach

Terrorist groups such as the Hezbollah and the al-Quaeda have built large infrastructures with cells in different countries and in several continents. Hezbollah has cells in Africa, Asia, Europe and USA The al-Quaeda has a global network. Around 1000 of OBL soldiers have infiltrated into Europe as per the German Secret Service, quoted in the Times magazine in October 2001. There have also been reports of al-Qaeda trying to link up with the Hezbollah in Lebanon, the Abu-Sayyaf in the Philippines; the Jemaah Islamiah are also linked to the al-Qaeda. It is now confirmed the bombings of the tourist resort in Bali was linked to al-Qaeda with the co-ordination of local terrorists.

The shift in the terrorist-motives has contributed to a change in the way some international terrorist groups are structured. Because groups based on ideological or religious motives may lack a specific political or nationalistic agenda they have no need for a hierarchical structure. Instead they can rely on loose affiliations with like-minded groups from a variety of countries to support their common cause. Al-Qaeda is the best known transnational terrorist organization. In addition to pursuing its own terrorist campaign, it calls on numerous militant groups that share some of its ideological beliefs to support its violent campaign against the US The more loosely affiliated these transnational terrorist networks are, the more difficult it is to predict, track and penetrate. They rely on a variety of sources for funding and logistical support including self-financing criminal activities such as kidnapping, narcotics, and petty crimes. Their networks of support include both front organizations and legitimate businesses and non-government organizations.

In India, the Pakistan based Lashkar-e-Taiba (LeT), the Harkat-ul-Ansar (HuA) and the Al Badr have so far been connected with terrorist activity in India. They are very much linked to the al-Qaeda and are members of the International Islamic Front for Jihad against the US. and Israel. They also describe their aims as the liberation of Kashmir from the control of Hindus and its merger with Pakistan, to be followed by the call for the creation of two more Muslim homelands, one for the Muslims in the North and other for the Muslims in the South of India. Two dangers associated with this group is that they have the ability to make attacks on American and Israeli targets in India to give vent to their anger against the above two nations and thereby causing embarrassment to the Indian Government. The second danger is a reality now.. These groups have managed to infiltrate their cadres into other parts of India and their presence is exists in the South as far as Tamil Nadu, Karnataka, Kerala and Andhra Pradesh.

The series of church blasts in Andhra Pradesh, Karnataka, Goa and Maharashtra between 21 May to 9 July 2000, by members of the Deendar Anjuman (a Muslim religious sect), in order to create chaos and communal tension, was believed to have been carried out at the behest of a Pakistan-based spiritual leader Syed Zia ul

Hassan of Deendar Anjuman. There have also been suggestions by foreign counter-terrorist experts that these groups were trying to get the support and assistance from the LTTE and its supporters in Tamil Nadu to train the cadres of the Al-Ummah and other Jehadi organizations in South India and providing them with material assistance. Al-Ummah had come into prominence on 14 February 1998 when they triggered off serial blasts in Coimbatore in which 65 people lost their lives but the main target Mr.L K Advani escaped by arriving late at the venue.

The terrorist attack at the Akshardham Temple in Gujarat occurred on the 24 September 2002. This was followed by the shooting of five dreaded terrorists in their hideout in M.S.Ramaiah Layout near Sanjaynagar in Bangalore on the 29 Sept 2002 and that made the terrorist threat perception even higher. The leader of the terrorists who were shot dead–Imam Ali had links with the ISI and the Hizbul Mujahideen and had trained in the use of explosives as far back as in 1990. He was also linked to the Al-Ummah and was the main person responsible for the bomb blast of the RSS headquarters in Chennai in August 1993 in which eleven people were killed. A mix of RDX and gelatine was used for the same. Imam had also plotted to assassinate Union Human Resource Development minister–Mr. Murli Manohar Joshi and the DIG of Coimbatore –Mr. Ashutosh Shukla. There also had plans to strike at famous temples in Tamil Nadu to disturb communal harm ony.

Further on the 9 November, 02 a cache of explosives which included 1200 electric detonators, 970 ordinary detonators, nine hand-grenades, 13 empty pipe bombs and 75 rounds of live ammunition, apart from explosive materials and chemicals used for making I.E.D's were seized from five Tamil ultras led by a person trained by People's Liberation Organization of Tamil Eelam. One does not know if there is any linkage of the above to r any other terrorist groups in the South or further to any transnational terrorist groups.

The cells through which terrorists carry out their activity usually consist of 5 or 6 people as seen above and the terrorists at times are globally networked and have been activated as and when required to carry out activities. For example on 11 April 2002, a tanker full of natural gas exploded outside the oldest synagogue of Djerba on the Tunisian Island Resort in which 16 people were killed. On 23 April 2002 the German police arrested nine members of Palestinian organizations suspected of plotting attacks. Hezbollah claimed responsibility for the attack on Israel-associated targets in Argentina as early as the 1990s.

However the cells are fast changing into groups of one and two, as we have seen during the past attacks in India. These cells interact with other cells. The primary function is for support functions such as recruitment, making money, moving men and material around (Often through criminal activity or linked to organized crime). Terrorist organizations also have links to organized crime syndicates and these syndicates frequently have access to, and have influence on political leaders. This makes such syndicates beneficial to terrorist groups that would seek to influence and intimidate. In return the organised crime syndicates can exploit terrorist campaigns for the power vacuum present in regions of instability as a paramilitary wing of the syndicate or to further coerce a weak government "to look the other way". If terrorists' interaction with transnational crime syndicates is successful the infrastructure of these interactions might be effective enough to provide terrorists with real opportunities for the introduction of weapons / explosives into a country. These cells also engage in looking for potential targets in different countries. At present terrorist groups are resorting to more indiscriminate attacks against "soft targets". The simplicity of these attacks might make them more difficult to predict and prevent. The more cells the better the chance of finding a good target. Targets are usually chosen based on scale, vulnerability and accessibility. Terrorists base their decisions to attack or not to attack on how vulnerable they perceive a target to be and thus how easy or difficult it would be to attack. Here perceived vulnerability and not just actual vulnerability matters. Accessibility is perhaps the single factor that determines who gets attacked and who doesn't.

2. Financing of Terrorist Activities

It is stated that most terrorist organizations manage to accumulate their wealth through charities and humanitarian organizations. Some organizations are unknowingly hijacked by terrorists who divert funds to finance their activities and others organizations proactively support terrorist groups. A recent report from the US Treasury Department acknowledged that terrorist activity is financed primarily through fund raising, and more often than not through legal non-profit organizations.

Charitable and humanitarian organizations have long been a preferred venue for terrorist financing with or without the knowledge of the organization or their donors. For example on December 14, 2001 federal officials in the U.S. raided the offices of the Global Relief Foundation (GRF) in Chicago and froze its assets. Days later, NATO forces raided GRF's offices in Kosovo after receiving credible information that the foundation was involved in planning attacks against US and European targets. GRF raised more than 5 million dollars in US alone last year. Although much of this funding perhaps went into legitimate causes, investigators maintain that GRF served as an important front for-al-Qaeda. There are other charitable and humanitarian organizations, which have also actively facilitated terrorist operations. For example, Mercy International Relief Organisation (MIRO) along with several similar groups played a central role in the 1998 US embassy bombings, in Africa. Several al-Qaeda members tried for their role in the above bombings named several charities as fronts for the terrorist group including MIRO. Other examples of terrorist front organization include the Holy Land Foundation for Relief and Development (funding HAMAS) and the al-Wafa organization (funding al-Qaeda). Funding of Terrorist activities in India could possibly be linked to the LeT which used to receive donations from the Al-Qaeda and also has its own organizational network in the form of schools, social service groups and religious publications. However there is no report or evidence to support this.

Now how does the Hotel Industry figure in all this? Does the Hotel Industry provide the Terrorist with the ingredients for an attack based on their aims, activities and their modus operandi? It is frightening but true.

Any Hotel has the following characteristics:

1. Multinational guest profile. On certain days, a particular Nationality in the form of groups or delegations could be more than the normal occupancy level.
2. Houses heads of states, ministers, government dignitaries etc.
3. Number of people at any given time could be very high especially on a weekend or on a busy evening, depending on the size of the hotel, its banquet functioning, the number of restaurants etc.
4. Easy accessibility.

These are visible targets where terrorists can avoid detection before and after the attack and further would also get maximum publicity. On the other hand hotels are also safe havens for terrorists to stay in.

In fact, in December 2000, an al-Qaeda operative was arrested in Jordan for his alleged role in a plot to blow up a hotel in Jordan filled with Americans and Israelis on New Year's Day. This sort of planning does not take time to turn into reality in India as we have seen with the intricate linkage of terrorist groups carrying out activities at the behest of others. This is also substantiated by the fact that the Americans and Israelis figure very much on their list of targets in their international Islamic Jihad. Not to mention other foreign nationalities cannot be discounted from the same as we have seen from the bomb blast in Bali.

At Present Terrorists in India have mainly confined their activities to:

1. Civilian targets in most cases to create communal disharmony. Example, Church attacks in the year 2000 was attempted to be blamed upon the RSS along with the attack on the Akshardham temple in Gujarat in 2002 and a number of other attacks in Jammu and Kashmir in which innocent civilians have been killed and also the attempted attack on the Ansal Plaza in Delhi.
2. Military targets in Jammu and Kashmir to create mass casualties to demoralize the Security Forces.
3. Hard targets like the attack on Parliament on 13 December 2001 and the attack on the Jammu and Kashmir assembly on October 2001.

In order to counter the terrorism-threat, hotels have to respond collectively (in terms of all the Hotels in the FHRAI). What is suggested is that in order to respond we will have to get information from the Police and Intelligence agencies about the Threat Assessment Levels existing in the country or in the state. This will also boil down to the threat or risk levels existing in individual hotels depending on the individual guest, groups, delegations, conferences etc. where a risk analysis has to be done to determine the risk levels associated with the same. This analysis is done based on the following parameters. Factors on which Guest Risk is determined:

- Guest Status / Designation–Head of State, Celebrity, CEO of company etc.
- Any dangers associated with Nationality
- Recognizing high security risk groups
- The government he / she belongs to.
- Police information
- Hit list category
- Threat assessment levels in the state / country.

Once the risk or threat level has been determined by the individual hotel then either independently or combined with the current threat assessment levels existing in the country/state, the threat condition has to be assigned. This threat condition should be classified into mainly four levels with different colour codes.

Severe	-	Red
High	-	Orange
Elevated /General	-	Yellow
Normal	-	Blue

Each threat condition level has to have its corresponding response strategies both in terms of prevention and precautionary measures, and on-site combating systems, which are carried out by the Hotel staff with the help and co-ordination of the police. Some may require the specialized services of certain organizations within the police and civil authorities, to ensure Security. Whatever the response strategy is, it should reduce if not eliminate the chances of terrorist activity against the hotel and at the same time also curb the impact on the hotel business if any.

In order not to embarrass or inconvenience the customer, all hotels which are part of the FHRAI have to meet and confer on the above and come out with a plan of action based on the above-mentioned guidelines. Once decided, the same can be informed to the guests. The guests must be informed that all the hotels in the Federation have adopted a new policy on security based on the current threat assessment levels and risk analysis of in-house guests residing in the hotel. Based on the above, threat condition levels will be assigned and accordingly preventive measures (which would have already been agreed upon by all hotels) will be carried out whether it be checking of all cars at the entrance, ban on cars entering the property or frisking of guests, r checking of bags etc. Each threat condition level and the measures to be taken have to be clearly defined and enforced on the guests, staff and visitors. Threat condition levels may or may not be similar for all hotels in the same city and should be co-coordinated by the individual unit security heads. These can also be informed to guest at the time of reservation and enforced accordingly.

All measures discussed above should be followed by all hotels in the Federation so that guests do not feel harassed or inconvenienced by some hotels which are doing it. It should be like the security at airports where any airport in India has the same security checks and procedures so that passengers quietly abide by them. Only thing in airports is that it is done daily but in hotels the frequency should be based on the threat condition levels which is decided by the security manager of the unit in consultation with his counterparts in other units and information received by the police and intelligence agencies.

In order to ensure the effectiveness of the above, the following factors should first be in place:

Information

At present the hotel industry is left to secure information through individual relationship with police and the intelligence organizations. There is no formal structure in place to access information, which can be acted upon depending on the adequacy of the validity, reliability and integrity of the information provider.

The challenge cuts across the gathering of preventive information as well as the reporting of facts after the occurrence of some event, which has threatened or resulted in a hotel security issue. The task is to set up an appropriate structure, along with the hotel Federation, the government and the civil authorities, to gather the necessary information.

In setting up sources they must be evaluated and then continuously monitored to ensure their validity, reliability and integrity since information of this nature must be correct and trustworthy.

One of the most difficult elements in accomplishing the above is getting access to information if it exists especially with respect to terrorism where the best intelligence agencies in the world have failed. In the case of crime it is relatively easier to access, gather and effectively communicate to all those responsible for hotel security.

In view of the above it is imperative that the hotel industry, in coordination with the government agencies, build up an effective structure for gathering and dissemination of information. This structure should define the channels, modes and standards for the transmission and sharing of all types of information pertaining to terrorist activity.

Internal Systems and Procedures

Internal systems and procedures need to be established to manage these terrorist threats, this is linked to a clear implication that these procedures must be constantly measured and reviewed both to judge their continued appropriation in a changing situations, and to ensure they remain effective agents for reducing losses and are relevant to changed circumstances. These would include screening of guests entering the hotel in order to spot any irregularities in their behaviour, gathering information from the front desk and housekeeping department during their period of stay in the hotel, access control measures, background checking of employees, patrolling etc. Standard security measures, and not just extraordinary ones, can have a major impact on us becoming potential targets.

These internal systems and procedures would also include:

(a) Decentralising the security function to make it the responsibility of all departments. The rationale for adopting this approach is to ensure that specific security duties belong to the designated non-security staff most able to ensure their completion. In addition each department manager must be accountable for the successful completion of those assignments. This further implies that different departments within the hotel jointly work together towards eliminating possible threats.

(b) Contingency planning is a must for all hotels to face the emerging new terrorist threats. This involves the formation of a Hotel Emergency Action Team "HEAT" to respond to the threats and emergencies in a planned and efficient way, which will not only save lives and minimize loss of property but will also demonstrate the hotel's commitment towards the safety of guests, employees and visitors. In this contingency planning process, each emergency should be separately addressed, with the duties and responsibilities of each member / department of the "HEAT" documented in detail. This planning should also be a group interaction so that a multitude of things including post-emergency management in the form of recovery and restoration are addressed. It is always smarter to have something and not need it than need something and not have it. It is only through such planning that training can be effectively conducted and much of the confusions frequently associated with emergencies can be reduced substantially. Contingency planning should include direction and control, communication, life safety, property protection, community outreach, and recovery and restoration.

(c) Training programmes for all levels of employees regarding what to look for and how to handle potential threats. This could also involve training to report any conversations with words like bombs, weapons, important government landmarks or if they happen to see drawings of important buildings or installations etc. This type of training will need to involve prevention activities / precautionary measures, which each department should be aware of and implement effectively.

Technology

In addition to the above two aspects of hotel security a greater investment is required in the field of technology in terms of security systems that will attempt to supplement internal systems and procedures and to enhance hotel security through methods of surveillance, access control, preventive and pos- event management.

(a) **CCTV:** One of the biggest technological hurdles that the hotel security industry will need to overcome this millennium will be in the area of compression technology. That is taking the picture from a CCTV camera and converting it to a digital format and then compressing it so that it can easily and quickly be transmitted and stored for extended periods. This will allow more for real time recordings of the digital systems and the better use of transmission technology. As computer technology continues to progress, artificial intelligence will continue to replace the human element in evaluating risk and reacting to situations. Instead of a security officer watching a monitor waiting to react to someone walking down a hall or climbing a wall, the monitor systems will handle the watch and alert the monitoring staff when it is time to look at the screen. They will also be given written / verbal instructions from the monitor as to how they should handle the situation.

(b) **Card Operated Locks:** Card operated locks are part of the electronic access control system which is being used for guest rooms in most modern hotels. These cards have no room number mentioned on them and are issued to a guest at the time of check-in. The card, after being programmed will include the identification of the cardholder and the time period in which to grant access to that particular room. The time the card was used and the identity of the cardholder will be recorded in the memory of the central processing unit and can also be printed for future reference. In the hotel industry the access to guest rooms is not limited to the guest only, as a number of staff provide ancillary services to the room and enter at different times. In case of thefts a printout can be taken from the lock to ascertain the number of entries and identities of the staff who went into that particular room. This definitely facilitates investigation and would lead to an apprehension of the culprit.

(c) **Intelligent Fire Detection Alarm System:** The Notified AM 2020, is one of the most advanced systems of fire detection. This system can display the detector location, type status and the value of smoke measurement for each of almost thousand detectors every few seconds. It also has a sophisticated voice system with remote audio amplifiers and a multiplex system with remote transponders that may function as standalone fire alarm panels.

(d) **Bomb Inhibitor:** The inhibitor system is made up of two components, which are the holding container and the inhibitor. The holding container consist of a plastic injection moulded and fitted with wall mounted brackets having a quick release drop lid offering access to the inhibitor. The inhibitor is an electromagnetic resin sealed in the welded sections fitted with two handles to allow for lifting over a suspected device. Its contents are 17 litres of non-toxic, heat suppressant chemicals including glycol and water. Inhibitors not only protect from explosions from up to 1 Kilogram of RDX but also contain the fire generated by the heat of the explosion.

(e) **Search Mirrors:** Search mirrors are used for checking cars.

(f) **Hand-Held Metal Detectors:** Mainly used for manual frisking to detect even small quantities of ferrous and non-ferrous metals carried by a person on his body.

(g) **Explosive Vapor Detectors:** Used to detect concealed and buried explosives by sniffing vapours. It analyses and indicates the presence of explosives, if any.

As we look into future, if hotels become a regular target for terrorist activities then the hotel industry will have to enhance their equipment and technology to counter these threats much in the same way as airports across the world have geared up in terms of technology.

The combination of all the three factors of information, internal systems and procedures, and technology will go a long way in reducing the threat of a terrorist attack. The direct impact of terrorism on the hotel industry (which is the fourth largest industry in India) and the travel industry is evident and it will not go away. Thus the hotel industry has to develop a collective response to the challenges of prevention and crisis management. Hotels also have to engage their own efforts to gather information, build networks, and do what they can to ensure a safe haven for its customers.

***

Technology in Fire Prevention

P Purkayastha

In recent times all over the world, several serious fire accidents have occurred in hotels resulting in large-scale loss of life and property. As a result of this, the hotel industry has been affected and many tourists intending to holiday prefer to choose motels and other such small establishments with a view to avoid experiences of holocaust of hotel fires which have been witnessed in many places, world over.

Another special feature of good hotels is their height as most of them are in high-rise buildings. This adds a new dimension to the fire safety problems. In India almost 50 hotels amounting to roughly 5% of the total HRBs of India have a 5-star rating. Amongst them almost 20% have been affected by fires of different magnitude sometime or the other. This is too big a loss-figure to be neglected by any safety professional.

The hotel fires, as per statistics, apart from property loss have caused deaths mostly by fire, smoke or toxic fumes. Many occupants, at the time of the fire accident have been trapped in the smoke-logged building and to save themselves, they have preferred to jump from windows or balconies and have crashed to their death.

Some case studies of fires have been compiled whose summary is shown in exhibit 1. The gist of the lessons from these fires should be pointers to every hotel establishment.

1. Delay in detection of fire.
2. Ventilation and ducting helped fire spread.
3. Escape route not planned.
4. No automatic fire alarm, and detection system defective or failure of fire alarm system during fire.
5. Fire dampers defective.
6. Direct opening through staircase: spread of fire and smoke could have been stopped by fire proof door on each floor.
7. Smoke created obstacle.
8. Locked exists, limited access and shortage of water supply to fight fire.
9. Interior finish, decoration, panelling increased fire load and helped fire spread.
10. Defective or no hydrant in hotels operating in HRB.
11. Electric short circuits.

Some special features that influence occurrence of fires in hotels are:

A. Frequent changes of occupants who may be unfamiliar with fire precaution, escape routes, and local languages.
B. Furnishing, lining, false ceiling, interior decoration etc. most of which are combustible and gives out lethal smoke when exposed to fire.
C. Various sources of inanition viz. kitchen, laundry, boiler room, Air Conditioner equipments, DG sets, furniture stores, etc.

For hotels operating in HRB the additional fire safety problems areas are:

(1) Height (2) Stack effect (3) Evacuation problem (4) Logistic problem (5) Fire load control (6) Capacity of public brigade areas ladder.

The factors influencing effective fire risk treatment is explained through Model A which identifies 3 important areas viz. Engineering, Enforcement and Education. The task of ensuring safety however can't be handled by a single agency.

The critical issues related to safety in hotels are

(a) Factors affecting the nature of flame spread.
(b) Rate of production of smoke and the time taken for a building of any size to be filled with smoke.
(c) Toxic effects on human body.
(d) Selection of proper in-house fire fighting, detection and alarm system.
(e) Maintenance of plants, air conditioner installations etc.
(f) Procedures for occupants /guests in hotels.
(g) Elements of fire prevention and emergency preparedness.

The fire hazard in a hotel is expressed by an equation:

F = f (N.A.H.D.P)
N = Number of occupants
A = Activities undertaken in the hotel viz. Heating and boiler installations, DG set, Swimming pool etc.
H = Height and area of the building occupied by the hotel.
D = Design and construction / fire load, surface, air rate available
P = Fire protection system, viz. hydrant, wet riser, communication system, air heating system.

Severity of Fire hazards Fs is given by:

Fs = F (L.T.V)
Fs = Severity of fire
T = Time within which fire operation starts

T = Duration of fire

V = Ventilation

Ventilation involves removal of smoke, gases and heat from the hotel building.

In case of a fire, the following measures must be taken:

(1) Protection of life by removing or diverting toxic gases and smoke from locations where building occupants must find temporary refuge.

(2) Improvement of environment in the vicinity of fire by removal of smoke and heat. This enables fire fighters to advance close to the fire and extinguish it with the minimum time, water and damage.

(3) Control of the spread and direction of fire by setting up air currents. This causes fire to be movedin a desired direction (occupants life and property can be protected).

Rf = F (Q.C.E.D.V)

Rf = Rate of flame spread

Q = Fuel composition, fire load degree of fire retardants.

C = Physical characteristics of material surface orientation, density, geometry, continuity.

E = Environmental factor, pressure, temperature, humidity, air velocity.

D = Direction of fire spread (doubling effect)

V = Ventilation.

The cloud which surrounds most fires is called SMOKE and consists of a mixed combination of groups such as:

(1) Hot vapours and gases given off by the burning material.

(2) Unburned decomposition and condensation matter.

(3) Air heated by the fire and entrained into the rising plume.

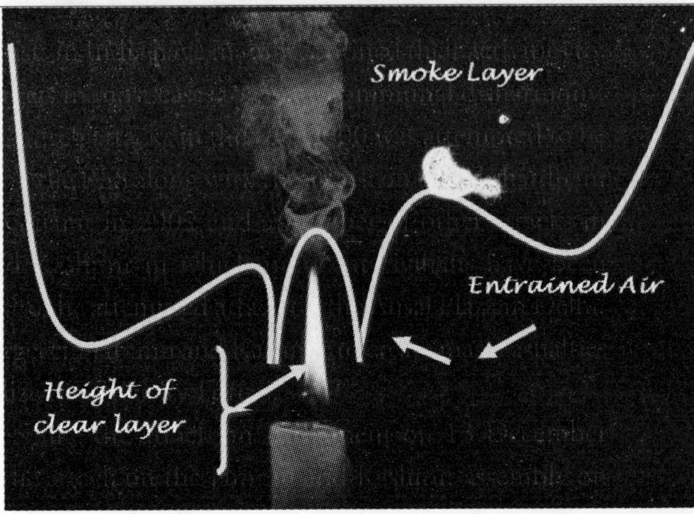

When smoke is generated, compared to the total volume of air entrained by the fire, the volume of fuel gases is small and it is therefore possible to establish that the rate of production of smoke by fire is approximately the rate at which the air is entrained and contaminated in the process of being used by the rising column of hot gases.

The rate of air entrainment will depend on:

(a) The perimeter of the fire.
(b) The heat output of the fire.
(c) The effective height of the column of hot gases above the fire (i.e. distance between the floor and the bottom of the layer of smoke and hot gases which form under the ceiling).

The rate of production of smoke in kg/ sec, M, is given by:

M = 0.096. P. Po. Y3/2 (G_10)
G = Acceleration due to gravity 9.81m/s^2
P = Perimeter of fire in meters
Po = Density of the ambient air (Kg / m^{3}at t. c.)
To = Absolute Temperature of flames in smoke plume K

Y = The distance from the floor to the lower surface of the smoke layer in meter. Similarly, time taken for building of any size to fill with the smoke = T seconds.

T = 20/Pg ½ (1/y ½ 1/*l* ½)

Where, A = floor area of building, room or compartment (m^2)

H = height of the building, room or compartment.

The contents of a hotel room can range from foam sofa, Television to wall paper designs etc.

The materials used for the above contain wood and pulp, polystyrene, PVC, polyethylene, wool, nylon, acrylic fibre, polyurethane, and urea-formaldehyde.

When burnt, toxic fumes are generated, they fall under two groups viz. pulmonary irritants (P) and systemic toxins(S)

Material		Harmful Product	Harmful concentration ppm air (30 min exposure)
1.	Wood and paper	CO (S)	4000
2.	Polystyrene	CO (S) (Styrone (S))	
3.	PVC	HCL (P) CO(S)	1000-2000
4.	Polyethylene	CO (S)	
5.	Wool, Nylon	HCN (S)	120-150
	Acrylic fibre	CO (S)	
	Polyurethane		
	Urea formaldehyde		

The elements of fire prevention and emergency preparedness are:

a.	Ignition	(a) Equipment and devices (b) Human accident (c) Vandalism and arson.
b.	Ignitable materials	(a) Fuel type and quantity (b) Fuel distribution (c) Housekeeping

c.	Emergency preparedness	(a) Awareness and Understanding (b) Plans of action: -Evacuation or temporary, storage -Self help extinguishment (c) Equipment (d) Maintenance – operating manual

The risks in a hotel could be identified as the following, based on case histories:

	Risks	Description
(i)	Careless smoking	Throwing cigarette butts in waste paper basket, carpet or on the bed; smoking in bed and not using ash tray.
(ii)	Electricity	Misuse of electricity, faulty electric appliances, plugging too many appliances in one socket, using room heater for drying clothes, unattended electric iron, defective wiring socket, gadgets, failure of insulation.
(iii)	Kitchen	Overheating, cooking oil/ fat, LPG leakage, heating appliances unattended.
(iv)	Laundry	Electric iron, drying m/c agents,
(v)	Intruders	Arson, malicious damage
(vi)	Contractor's worker	welding, painting and repairs.

To counter the risks, proper management action plans should be designed:

Action Plan

1. Clear instruction to the guests should be given through notice as to what guests should do upon noticing a fire.
2. To provide automatic fire detection and alarm system that can be heard at all places preferably through a public address system.
3. Providing adequate number of portable fire extinguishers and fuel protection system.
4. To train staff in fire fighting.

Procedures

1. Guests to be handed a safety card showing safety instructions and means of escape.
2. Restriction of number of persons to be admitted in certain specific areas like banquet hall, to be imposed.
3. Plans should be displayed at corridor near landing / stairs / lift, showing escape routes, locations of telephone, fire alarms points, extinguishers etc.
4. Proper lighting in corridors and stairways and exit signs along the escape routes should be provided.
5. Activities like welding, cutting, boiling of bitumen etc. must to be done under supervision.
6. Occupants should be warned to unplug TV/ heaters etc. when no one is in the room.

Maintenance and House Keeping

1. Corridors, passages, fire, emergency exists, and escape routes should be kept unlocked and free from obstruction.
2. All electric appliances / switches should be checked regularly.
3. Communication equipments should be in good working condition.
4. Signs should be clearly visible.
5. Chimneys and fuels should be inspected and cleaned.
6. Ventilation and ducts should also be periodically checked.
7. A.C. plant's checking should be done regularly.
8. Boiler and water-heating equipment checking should be done.
9. There should be daily or weekly tests of fire detection and alarm system.
10. Wet riser system including hose reels and branch pipe should be inspected.
11. Portable extinguishers should be checked.

Exhbit 1 Inicdents of Hotel Fire

No	Month/Date	Description	Death & Injury
1	7.12.46	Wineoff Hotel, Atlanta USA, HRB (15+2) Cause undetected	119 dead and 65 injured
2	14.11.77	Filipinas Hotel, Manila Philippines, HRB.	47 dead, large number injured
3	June 1978	Hotel Stadhotell, Boras, Sweden, Cigarette thrown in waste paper basket	20 dead and 60 injured
4	19.10.78	Hotel Oberoi Mount Everest, Darjeeling, India Fire at Lunchroom	No death + Rs. 15 lac property loss
5	18.1.79	Grand Hotel, Calcutta, Electric Short Circuit	No death + Rs. 4 crore loss
6	12.7.79	Hotel Carona de Aragon, Zaragoza, Spain, HRB, overheating of oil in frying pan	85 death + injury
7	21.11.80	MGM Hotel,	Las Vegas USA HRB84 dead + 679 injured
8	1.1.86	Dupont Plaza, USA, HRB Kitchen	97 dead + 140 injured
9	23.1.86	Hotel Siddarth Continental, India, Banquet Hall (HRB)	37 died + 46 injured
10	5.9.86	Hotel Kristiansand, Norway HRB, Electrical fault	34 dead + 50 injured
11	27.1.2008	Fire at Grand Hotel, guests evacuate five-star hotel in Vasant Kunj, New Delhi, India	A fire service official suffered some injuries, while the guests and hotel staff managed to escape unhurt
12	9.12.2011	Kolkata AMRI hospital, The fire spread fast from the basement of the hospital, engulfing one ward after the other and trapping hundreds of people.	89 patients including three hospital staffers lost their life in the incident. Out of the 150 admitted patients in the hospital, 90 were rescued.

Exhibit 2

Specimen Notice to Guests

Fire Instructions

If you discover a fire:

Raise the alarm by --

The nearest fire alarm call point to the room is at------------------

----

If you hear the fire alarm:

Leave route room immediately and proceed to the assembly point at-----------------------------by the nearest available exit.

Your primary escape route is ------------------------------------, and the alternative route is --------------------------

Close the door of your room and any other which you use.

Do not:

Use the lift as a means of escape

Shout or run: this tends to cause panic ------------------------------

----

Study the notice carefully.

Exhibit 3

(To be displayed in public areas and guest rooms)

Fire Prevention Recommendations For Guests

1. The porter showing you your room will indicate the ordinary as well as the emergency passages, particularly the escape routes in case of fire.
2. Find out the nearest escape route(s) from your room. Locate fire alarm, countdown to exit and note halfway obstacles immediately after check in.
3. Carrying and using materials and liquid constituting a fire hazard are not allowed.
4. Electric equipment must not be adjusted or altered without the

prior permission of the management.

5. Do not smoke in bed. Do not throw stubs into the waste paper basket or through the window. Extinguish them in the ashtray.
6. Upon the outbreak of fire, or if you smell smoke, please notify the switch board at once by lifting the receiver of your telephone. Please indicate clearly the number of your room and your observation.
7. Do not act rashly and do not expose yourself to any unnecessary danger by leaving your room, you might be safer in your room than anywhere else. Try to stay in your room if the door is hot and the hallway smoky. Open the door only if it is cool.
8. In case of fire don't leave using lift; use the staircase.
9. On leaving the room, shut all window and doors to avoid any draught. Don't walk through smoke. Crawl and keep moving along the wall on the exit side.
10. If fire brigade appears, follow their instruction.
11. Use wet sheets and towels to block smoke creeping in through doors and vents.
12. If smoke fills the room, open the window and shout for help.
13. Don't jump from above 1st floor.

Panic is more dangerous than fire; so remain calm and think.

***

Use of CCTV in Security

Charlie R A Pierce

Education is an ongoing process of feeding the mind information, sorting that information and then applying it in a productive manner. It should never be the endeavour of an individual to memorize everything about anything. It should instead be the goal of all professionals to learn how and where to find, quickly, the answers and information needed.

With CCTV, as with any technical field, you should avoid the temptation of learning a vast number of model numbers and manufacturer's symbols. This language is often confusing and instead of making you knowledgeable, it usually leaves you or intimidated of your market. Knowing these things simplifies your job and gives you true power of knowledge. Model numbers do when it comes to the complexities of making things work in a productive and efficient manner.

As it is true in any adventure, the best is yet to come. In the world of CCTV, we have yet to make our mark on society. I challenge each person reading this book and/or attending one of our training seminars, to reach out with the fullest portion of their imagination and make a new mark in the world. Likewise, I pass on a small warning to those individuals that reach out through CCTV. It is our responsibility to keep the world safe. It is likewise our responsibility to respect those virtues that have made our nation the greatest in the world. Privacy is a right and should be carefully preserved. As our industry produces smaller cameras, lenses, and other peripheral equipments, it becomes very easy to cross the line between security and trespassing. It is the responsibility of our industry as well as of us independently to conserve freedom and privacy.

CLOSED CIRCUIT VIDEO

Taking the Mystery out of Closed Circuit Video

For years have everyone has been intimidated by closed circuit television video (CCTV). Sales people are to suggest simple systems because of all the numbers and fancy names surroundings the equipment. Installers avoid hook-ups because of the different types of cables and connections and the need of explaining the final product to the customers. Service people are afraid to service CCTV systems because the customers may ask them a question they can't answer.

It has been an assumption of many that CCTV is complicated and too intense for a person of average intelligence to master, and so this greatest of all security fields has been held at a distance for many years.

Although this manual is not trying to produce service technicians, it is important to make the sales personnel, installers, and field service persons, aware of the simplicity of the basic system.

In order to properly design, install and/or maintain any CCTV system, a few theories and operations of the cameras, monitors and peripheral equipments must be learned. Although it seems like a major project, this information can be learned with a minimal amount of effort and in a relatively short period of time.

At the same time, it should be understood by any person who has the ability to plug in a toaster can install a camera, cable, and monitor and have it work. It is not an operation and monitor response is the purpose of the learning.

To remove the first cloud of mystery surrounding closed circuit video, you must realize that, like many other things in our lives, video is nothing more than a man-made illusion. The illusion is that what is seen on the monitor as a moving free flowing picture with no breaks is nothing more than a sequence of individual pictures flashed in front of the eye at a rate that the brain perceives as motion.

Just like movie film in the theatre or some home movies, closed circuit video is made of individual pictures divided by periods of blank, dark screen, but it is minus the film. We know that if anything is flashed in front of human eyes at a specific rate or speed in the case of CCTV, 60 times per second, the brain will perceive a single unit versus individual items. Adding a blank between pictures finishes the illusion and adds smoothness to what is being viewed.

The monitor paints individual lines across the screen one at a time from top to bottom. The total combination of these horizontal lines is called resolution. The more lines on a screen, the better or sharper the video picture appears. Most monitors and cameras work in a two to one interface pattern. This is where the monitor paints the old-numbered lines of resolution first and then comes hack and re-sweeps the screen in the even-numbered paths. This process creates 60 fields of information per second. Odd fields and even fields combine to make up one complete frame or picture of video. Therefore, there are 60 fields or 30 complete frames flashed each second before our eyes.

The end of the First Misery of CCTV

Video pictures are not free flowing but are a series of individual pictures flashed before our eyes at a rate of 60 pictures per second with a blank moment between each picture.

System Breakdown-Peice by Piece

The second great mystery surrounding closed circuit is hidden amongst great piles of literature written about hundreds of pieces of equipment needed to design, install, and/or a video system. This literature tends to hide the fact that a closed circuit video system consists of three parts. Anything else that may be needed in the system is considered a peripheral piece and will fall into its category in a systematic manner.

The three parts of any video system, regardless of how intense it may appear, are the camera unit (used to transform a reflected light image to electronic signal), coaxial cable (wire used to transmit the electronic video signal from the camera to the monitor), and a monitor (unit used to translate the electronic video signal received from the camera via the coaxial cable into a electronic picture on a screen).

All other parts of the system will fall into several simple categories:

1. If it makes the camera move, it will be a Pan or Pan/tilt unit. Pan moves the unit mounted to it from side to side. Pan/tilt moves the unit mounted to it from side up and down.
2. If it commands a function of the pan or pan/tilt, or atomic lens, it will be a controller. Controllers fall into separate categories of lance controller, pan or pan/tilt controller, or operations controller which is a combination of the first two in a single unit.
3. If it all allows several cameras to be monitored on a single or multiple monitors either in sequence, or one air a time, it will fall into the category of switcher. Video switchers enhance a video system, allowing it to save costs while remaining effective through multiple cameras monitoring through a single source of view.
4. If it forces into a chip or tube within cameras, it will fall into the category of lances. Lances come in a variety of sizes, allowing great choices for area views.
5. If it allows the video signal to be transmitted via any source (cable, phone line, radio waves, light waves, etc), it will be a video transmitter and/or receiver.

6. If it makes the video signal stronger or bigger for long-distance runs, it will be an amplifier.
7. If it retains the video information on magnetic tape, wire or electronically, it will be a video recorder of some sort.

Once a simple understanding of the basics in each category is achieved, it becomes possible to completely design a simple or major system on paper and have it work in the field. Each category has its own rules and guidelines and each point of the CCTV system may be approached individually as the need arises.

Camera Tube and CCD Comparisions

When comparing results of different types of tubes and chip cameras, it must keep in mind each tube and/or chip was designed for a specific application. If a few simple rules are kept in the forefront when designing and/or installing a system, the amount of cost savings, as well as a better performance, can have dramatic effect.

1. Slandered vision tubes are designed to work in full, even, constant, and light. A typical example of a good application for the slandered vision tube would be a well-lit office area with few windows or north-exposure windows.
2. Ultricon and newvicon are tube-type cameras designed to work in lower levels of light and require an auto-iris lens. Typical applications are receptionist areas with windows causing varying light due to opening lower lit parking ramps, outside ATM windows; etc.
3. Charged Coupled Device (CCD) or chip cameras are solid state cameras designed to work in a large variety of applications. Because they have no tube to do image reproduction, they are immune to many problems of past CCTV cameras, such as: blooming, heavy maintenance from tube wear, heat, size, etc. They have inherent problems of their own, such as: picture smear, less sensitivity and loss of horizontal resolution.

CCTV Camera Tube and CCD Characteristics

CAMERA TYPE	LIGHT TYPE	A/1 LENS	IR SENSITIVE	RESOLUTION	LAG TIME	BURN IMAGE	EXPECTED TUBE LIFE
STANDARD VIDICO	FULL CONSISTENT33.3 FL	NO	LOW 700 TO 775 NH. AVERAGE	GOOD 600 LINES TYPICAL	LOW FAST RESPONSE	FAIRLY EASY ESP/ LOW LIGHT	I TO 5 YR DEPENDS ON LOCATION
UL TRICON*	LOW/FULL VARIABLE.029 -.03 FL	YES ALWAYS	HIGH 1050 TO 1200 NM. AVERAGE	GOOD 550 LINES UP	LOW QUICK RESPONSE	GUARANTEED NO	1 TO 2 YR DEPENDS ON LOCATION
NEWVICON*	LOW/FULL VARIABLE.04 -.43FL	YES ALWAYS	FAIR 850 TO 900 NM. AVERAGE	GOOD 550 LINES UP	MEDIUM SLOW RESPONSE	FAIRLY EASY ESP/ BRIGHT LIGHT.	1 TO 2 YR DEPENDS ON LOCATION
SIT	VERY LOW ½ MOON.00002FL	YES ALWAYS	LOW 650 TO 700 NM. AVERAGE	FAIR 500 LINES TYPICAL	FAIR DAY MED-NITE FAST RESP	POSSIBLE BUT VERY DIFFICULT	1-YEAR
C MOS CCD	CONSISTENT.25 - 5FL	DEPENDENT UPON APPLICATION	HIGH 1050 TO 1300 NM. AVERAGE	AVERAGE 425 LINES UP	NONE	GUARANTEED NO	5 YEAR AVERAGE
INTERLINE CCD	LOW/FULL VARIABLE .035 -.04FL	DEPENDENT UPON APPLICATION	HIGH 1050 TO 1300 NM. AVERAGE	AVERAGE 425 LINES UP	NONE	GUARANTEED NO	5 YEAR AVERAGE
FRAME TRANSFER CCD	LOW/FULL VARIABLE .03-.035FL	DEPENDENT UPON APPLICATION	LOW 700 TO 850 NM. AVERAGE	AVERAGE 425 LINES UP	NONE	GUARANTEED NO	5 YEAR AVERAGE

SIT, ISIT, ICCD cameras are designed to work in extreme low light conditions. Because of this design, they will produce grainy or less detailed day pictures than their counterparts; Ultricon, Newvicon, CCD, SIT, and ISIT cameras are very seldom necessary in well-lit parking lots. Typical applications are outside parameters where lighting is normal, back-side of factories where lighting may not be very strong, parking lots where lighting is minimal, far-reach fence boundaries and outreaching properties surrounding a site.

Comparing Camera Sensitivities

Choose the proper camera for any video system, there are several considerations that must be into account before any final decisions can be made as to the type of camera and the size of lance used. They are as follows:

(a) The overall sensitivity of the camera needed based upon the actual application.

(b) The amount of light available at the scene (scene illumination) as measured on the low end then the conversion of that information into reflection light standards.

(c) The purpose of the proposed video picture. Is it to identify the subject or detect change or motion?

(d) The type and size of lance that will he needed and the effect that the lens will have on the camera as far as low end sensitivity is concerned.

For the purpose of this article, we will be discussing the first two and what they mean to you the signer, dealer, or end user.

The first consideration in overall camera sensitivity has to do with the various light levels that will allow a camera to produce a good picture. Since all cameras will produce a picture in full, bright light, the contest here would be picture clarity or quality. However, the true contest of camera comparisons usually comes in the lower light levels. Parking lots at night under minimum lighting conditions, the perimeters of properties such as gates and fences at night, inside warehouses and other poorly lit areas, these are the places where a camera's "sensitivity" is really tested, and each manufacturer claims to have the best camera for the job. The first place to determine the camera's sensitivity is the manufacturer's specification (spec) sheet. All manufactures list their camera's sensitivity based upon the minimum amount of light required in a scene (scene illumination). This listing, however, can be deceptive to the CCTV designer since cameras do not see light as measured from the source. They do see what is known is reflective light. Just as your eyes do not see the light passing through space and air, neither does a camera. What your eye and the camera do actually see is the light that is bounced off an object. Knowing that cameras view reflective light versus straight light is extremely important to the designer; this is because all things, and colours, reflect different amounts and types of light.

Let's break this down a little further. White light (visible light) is composed of seven different colours of equal intensity but different wave lengths. These seven colours make up the visible light spectrum and can most easily be re-merged with the help of a simple acronym, "ROY G. BIV". Spelled out, this acronym goes as follows: R-Red, O-Orange, Y-Yellow, G-Green, B-Blue, I-Indigo, V-Violet. The reflective characteristics of various materials determine what the average eye or camera will see and at what intensity. As soon as I absorb any one colour within the visible light spectrum, my eye or camera perceives a different colour. A good example of this world is a red rose. A red rose will reflect only the red light waves of the visible light that strike it. The other entire colour is actually absorbed, creating the illusion to the eye (or camera) that the rose is red. A black asphalt parking lot absorbs all of the seven colours in the visible light spectrum and therefore appears black. In actuality, black is the absence of reflective light. All this information is very good and I realize that almost everyone learned it in the fourth grade. I also realize that you are probably asking yourself why I have bothered to write about it. It is very important to understand the effect of various lighting connections within a CCTV system as it is designed. This knowledge could save you hundreds of dollars and hours of frustration.

Since a camera is designed in a way that it reproduces its images from reflected light, the amount and type of reflected light needed to produce a video image is what determines the sensitivity of the cameras, not the actual scene illumination. Your CCTV system designs depend, therefore not only on the amount of light available at the scene, but also on the amount of reflected light based upon what you are watching. Since CCTV jobs are often installed in a multitude of environments, each individual environment must be considered as far as scene reflectance is concerned. A good example of this would be to compare blacktop pavement to snow. Which of the two has the higher reflectance levels? Obviously, the snow does. To help in the determination of average reflective levels of various objects and colours, the following chart may be used.

**** Light Reflectance Chart****

Asphalt	(black)	5% reflectance
Concrete	(New)	40% reflectance
	(Old)	25% reflectance
Red brick		25% reflectance
Grass (green)		40% reflectance
Face (Caucasian)		18% to 25% reflectance
Snow		95% reflectance

More detailed information on different, average reflective values of materials and colours can be found in any good book about 35mm photography. To apply this information in a way that means something to you in your CCTV system's designs you need to think about it like this:

If I have five "units of light" available to me in a parking lot at night, how much actual reflective light does my camera have to work with? The answers are very easily calculated using the previously mentioned light reflectance chart. Since asphalt has a 5% reflectance value, the formula would look like this: 5 units of light (available) X.05 (scene's average reflective value) =.25 units of actual usable light, in other words, the actual amount of light that my camera can put to use based upon my original finding of 5 units of light (scene illumination), which my manufacturer's spec sheet led me to believe to be important. I would have been greatly disappointed when the camera was installed. After the final calculation of scene reflectance, I now know that my camera needs to have a sensitivity rating of at least.25 units of light or less for its low end in order to produce a favourable picture at night.

The next step is to translate our "units of lights" into an actual working terminology such as "FOOTCANDLE" (fc), or "LUX" (lx) or FOOTLAMBERTS (ft), for now, I will define each of the above like this: one fc of light is the amount of light that can be measured on a one foot square area, one foot away from the light of candle. One lx of light is the metric conversion of fc and can be equated as 1 lx=.0929 fc, or, for the purpose of this article, rounded out to 1 lx=.1 fc. One fc is the amount of light that a candle actually produces as measured as an output of the flame at a distance of one foot.

Since all manufacturers use one of these variables for description of camera sensitivity, we will use them in our future examples instead of "units of light".

Example: I need to choose a camera that has enough sensitivity to view the back area of my building at night. I have approximately 2 fc of light overall at the darkest time the area that I am viewing mostly contains grass (green). Based upon the reflectance chart, grass has a 40% reflectance value. How much actual reflected light do I have and what is the true sensitivity needed from my camera?

Do the following: 2 fc (available light) x.4 (reflectance value) =.8

fc reflective light. Therefore, I will need a camera that has enough sensitivity to work in.8 fc of light. I can find that number on the manufacturer's spec sheet under camera sensitivity.

Now that true lighting has been discussed, a few key points about reading manufacturer spec sheets should be gone over. At many of my seminars around the country, I have asked a simple question looking for a show of hands in response. "How many people in the room feel that manufacturers lie on their camera spec sheets when it comes to camera sensitivity?" It never ceases to amaze me that the overwhelming majority of people that I ask this question feel that all manufacturers lie or cheat on the spec sheet. I'm here to tell you that they don't, they can't. If they did they could be sued or arrested for false advertisement. If this is a fact, which it is, then how come there are so many times when something does not perform in the field, the way it does on paper? Primarily, because reading a spec sheet is almost an art. If I can't lie on paper, what can I do to make my product appear the best? I can 'blow smoke' or write the facts in such a way that they appear great. This is the subject that we will be covering in the next few paragraphs.

There are probably twenty different ways in which I can write something and each way will make it sound different. For example, read the following statement out loud put the emphasis of your voice on the italicized word each time you say it. "I am great! - I am great!" as you noticed. Each time you changed the inflection point of the sentence, the meaning of the sentence also changed slightly. The same theory is used when writing spec sheets. If I use different terms, the facts don't change, but the way information is perceived could. For instance, foot candle (fc) versus lux (lx). As stated earlier in this article, foot candle is nothing more than a measurement of light and lux (lx) is the metric conversion of it. Suppose you have designed a camera that will produce a picture in 1.5 lx of light. Wouldn't your spec sheet make the camera sound more sensitive if you instead wrote that your camera would produce a picture in.14 fc of light? Of course another case might be that all your competitors use the term foot-candle on their spec sheets and you would like to make it a little more different to compare your camera to theirs. Wouldn't you use lux then? I might.

A second trick that you might use would depend upon your camera's ability to see or react to infrared (IR) light. Light is measured by wavelength. The measurement used for light is nano-meter (nm). One nm= 1 billionth of a meter. A violet light wave is 400 nm long. A green light wave is 550 nm long and red is 700 nm long. All cameras react differently to different wavelengths or colours of light. Some cameras have the ability to see in light that is invisible to our eyes. This is infrared light and is measured from 700 nm to 1100 nm and up. Once we pass the 1200 nm mark, this light is actually heat, the same type of heat that you cook your dinner with or warm your room with. Some cameras have the ability to see this IR light, in the same way as you or I would see visible light. As a matter of fact, different colours and surfaces reflect IR light much more profusely than visible light. Green reflects 95% of all IR light. That is why green grass feels cool, even on a bright sunny day versus a brown dirt road.

To give a better example of what IR lighting might do for my camera's picture, imagine a dark room with a single bulb producing infrared light. To you and me, the room would be pitch-black and we would not be able to see our hands in front of our faces. To the right camera, however, it would be like daylight in the room and it will be able to see in great detail. So what does this have to do with your new camera's spec sheet? Plenty! You have designed a camera that is sensitive to the IR light scale. All cameras are tested using a bright light against a reflective surface. As this light is blacked out, the camera's video signal is measured until it is below a usable level. If this camera is sensitive to IR lighting (heat), what would happen if it were tested using a very hot lighting system. As the visible light was cut back dramatically, the heat produced by the bulbs would remain consistent or drop in much smaller proportion to the visible light. Therefore this camera would continue to produce a usable picture in levels well below the visible light levels of the real world. So, to really compare cameras on an apples to apples level, I must know the heat levels of the lamps that are used to test the cameras for specification purposes. This is very seldom printed by anyone and it should be noted that all cameras should be tested with "cold" light (non-heat producing sources) such as fluorescent ones.

A third approach that you could take with your newly designed camera would be to play with the reflectance value of the light used to test your camera. For example, your camera has a low end sensitivity of.14 fc. This is based upon using a light source but if you increased the reflectance value of the test surface to 90% (almost slow), wouldn't your spec-sheet come out sounding even better? Of course it would! You just increased the sensitivity (or light) by 20%. Now your camera would have a low end sensitivity rating of.112 fc or rounded out,.11 fc.

A fourth step that you could take to make you cameras seem even more sensitive would be to publish the "imager illumination". This is the amount of reflected light that is actually needed to produce a picture based upon the tube or chip requirements after the lens. In other words, it is the light that is actually focused upon the imager. Although there are some within the industry who swear that this as the only true way to measure a camera's sensitivity, there are still a few variables that tend to make comparisons impossible. In other words, this is another example of a lot of smoke! The first step towards improving this number is to use a lens with the least amount of light loss or the fastest lens available. Until recently, this has been a lens with an f-stop (focal stop) or iris opening of f-1.4 the formula to reach this point is as follows: reflected light (lx or fc) X.14 = imager illumination. In other words, your camera now has imager illumination sensitivity of.0196 fc. (.14 fc scene illumination X.14 f-stop=.0196 imager illumination sensitivity). Sounding better all the time! Until recently, this has not been a major problem. Only a few manufacturers used f-1.4 iris opening. However, because of the decreased sensitivity of the CCD (charged coupled device) chips over the tubes of yesteryears, the lens industry has reacted favourably by developing faster lenses. Now it is possible to purchase lenses with f-stops of f-.8 or less. Unfortunately, it is not possible to use these lenses on all cameras, and their focal lengths are limited. The point is this: what if you now test your camera with a lens having an f-stop of.8 instead of f-1.4 you have just increased the ability of the lens to pass light by 42.5% you can write your spec sheet (honestly) as having an even more sensitive lower end. Even through you may not be able to use these wide aperture lenses in the real world at this point, it doesn't really matter. You've not lied about the camera; you've just done a good job of selling it. YIKES! The two previous examples would now read that the cameras minimum scene illumination needs would be.063 fc (based upon f-.8 at 90% reflectance) and its imager sensitivity would now be.0112 fc. (.14 fc scene illumination X.08f-stop =.0112 fc imager illumination sensitivity).

The range of possible spec listings for this hypothetical camera as discussed so far includes:

Scene Illumination: 1.4 Lux Or.14 Foot Candles
(Based upon 75% reflectance at f-1.4)
Scene Illumination: 1.1 Lux Or.11 Foot Candles
(Based upon 90% reflectance at f-1.4)
Scene Illumination:.63 Lux Or.06 Foot Candles
(Based upon 90% reflectance at f- 8)
Scene Illumination:.19 Lux Or.02 Foot Candles
(Based upon 90% reflectance at f- 1.4)
Imager Illumination:.11 Lux Or.011 Foot Candles
(Based upon 90% reflectance at f-.8)

So you ask me, "Which listing should I print?" they all mean about the same amount of baloney, but some sound better than others. Remember, we haven't lied about the true sensitivity of our camera; we just haven't printed anything that is usable to the designer at the table or in the field. The final word is that all cameras should be tested and compared (side-by-side) to each other in all applications where a showdown of sensitivity is necessary.

The worst part of it all is that we haven't even sparked upon some of the newer approaches to spec sheet painting. What if, in writing a spec sheet for our imaginary camera, I wasn't satisfied with the final outcome of any of the numbers as listed previously? I could then use another approach. I would list the sensitivity of my camera based upon "usable video". Usable video (UV) is another way of saying- this is the absolute bottom amount of light needed before my camera will not produce a picture at all. Dependent upon the heat of the test lamp, the sensitivity of the camera to IR lighting, and the amount of actual video signal that the camera is able to produce, I can create a very snowy, noisy, and generally grainy video picture by working in light levels below the necessary minimum. Even through this picture is below grade. I can print my new findings as true minimum sensitivity for the "usable video". In other words, if you really don't care about the overall quality if the picture, my camera will now work in light levels anywhere from 20% to 45% than the posted "full video" camera sensitivity. Have I lied? No, I just didn't bother to tell you that USABLE VIDEO is not necessarily a clean, clear picture.

Another good one is the listing "With AGC on" or "Without AGC" AGC stands for auto gain circuit or auto gain control. All cameras that are mounted outside should have the AGC in the "on" position. This is an internal video amplifying system that works to maintain the video picture and tends to degrade the overall video picture somewhat. It is extremely useful when the camera swings into an area that is just below the required minimum light requirements. It allows the security person to continue viewing is areas that normally would go totally black. It should never be used as a measurement of the camera's sensitivity. The sensitivity rating listed under the "AGC on" column is another way of saying usable video. It is another smoke screen used to make cameras appears, on paper, more sensitive than what they are.

This section is adapted from an article written by C. Pierce appearing in the March, 1991 issue of "Access Control Magazine".

CCD Explanations and Attributes

CCD or "chip" cameras have been available since the early fifties. However, they were not developed enough, until the late 80s and early 90s to have a major impact on the industrial closed circuit video market.

CCD stands for "CHARGED COUPLED DEVICE". This device is a small photosensitive, solid state unit that has been developed to replace the imager or tube in the closed circuit camera. It was originally developed for this purpose many years ago, but proved to be ahead of its time electronically. Because of its complexity, it was not cost-effective to reproduce and would not enter the market and masses until several years after the consumer market developed it through the "CAMCORDER".

Like its counterpart the tube, the CCD comes in a variety of sizes or formats. The most common of these in the market today are the ½", 1/3", and 2/3". A chip has been developed, which was originally the new hope for a very sensitive type unit that could replace some of the very low light tubes in the market today. It proved however, to be more a case of a larger chip versus more sensitive one. The similarity of format sizes between the tube and the chip are the only comparisons that can be made between the two technologies and will be needed as reference for the purpose of lens selection. From that point on, the two have absolutely no true electronic comparisons.

When the CCD chip is combined with microcircuits and surface-mount technology, the manufacturer is able to produce cameras as small as one square inch. There are major drawbacks oftheir new micro sized cameras, however involves lenses' sensitivity and video carrier connections.

Lenses being what they are today are not easily shrunk due to the complex process of light refraction needed to produce a good and usable video image. This situation is being rectified quickly, and the next few years is likely to show improvements in the area of lens development.

The second factor, sensitivity, is very important. The more sensitive a camera the lower or less light is required on a scene to produce a good video picture. Since the average chip is not as sensitive as its counterpart, the easiest solution is to produce lances that have lower f-stop functions. This only means that the iris within the lances can open and the optics can pass light more efficiently, allowing for less light loss before the image or chip. If the chip can't be made more sensitive, give it more light. This simple solution will have a strong effect on the chip camera's ability to replace the tube in all situations.

The third point of video, power and lens connections to the cameras themselves is being aware when designing a system and choosing equipment that will indeed connect to the camera and ensuring that the power supply for the camera is of the proper style, voltage and design.

Chip cameras also open up old worlds of colour. Although colour has been available in closed circuit video through tubes for several years, it has been extremely costly and inefficient. Colour tubes are expensive and short lived. They also have burn (retained images) and auto white balance problems. It must be remembered however that colour pictures are extremely dependent upon lighting conditions. Therefore black and white chip cameras can outperform colour cameras in lower light situation. This limits colour applications to indoor locations or where lighting can be controlled outside. Some lower light colour chip cameras are available in the market, but they are computer enhanced and will not produce full motion in extreme lighting conditions. By full motion, I refer to a full sixty frames, or thirty fields of video pictures per second.

Another, and perhaps a greater, advantage of the chip over the tube pertains to life expectancy. The tube camera's expected life (ability to produce a favourable picture) depends upon the type of tube, installation conditions, and the actual field of view that was prominent for the camera. A standard video tube has an average life expectancy of 3 to 5 years while the lower light Ultricon and Newvicon tubes look forward to a short 2 year average. The CCD chip can last for an average of 5 years or longer before any deterioration of picture creeps in. This means that the camera can be cost effectively replaced at the end of its life cycle, versus re-chipped.

With the development of the chip camera, many of the old terminology and problem situations common to tube cameras have also been left by the wayside.

Advantage of the Chip Over Tube

1. The tube cameras had an inherent problem with burned or retained image. This would happen when a camera was installed in a fixed location with too much or too little (dependent upon the type of tube) light. The target area of the tube (the photosensitive material where the light is focused) would become permanently damaged. This damage was an actual desensitizing of the target area in direct proportions with light that was focused on it. The end result was a picture, of the area that the camera was located. The most common system of this symptom of this was a picture that had ghosting. It appeared that the solution to this problem was to replace the tube. The chip, because of its electronic design and solid state material,

does not have the ability to burn or retain the image. Therefore, it will outlast a tube in most situations and create a clean crisp picture over longer periods with less intolerance to lighting conditions. The major concern here is: If the light is intense enough to burn your eye (such as extremely hot light created by welding) it will burn or damage a tube or chip if proper filters or precautions are not taken in advance.

2. Tube cameras are large, bulky and create a lot of heat. The size is relevant to several different factors ranging from the size of the tube, the amount of circuitry needed for the high voltage section (used to power the tube), and the board mounted circuit pieces to run the camera. The heat from a tube camera is generated from two points. The normal circuitry within the camera is a small part of the problem. The major amount of heat within the tube style camera comes from the filament within the tube. A filament is used to heat the cathode within the electron gun of the tube. This works well enough for the tube, but produces the negative side effect of making the cameras run hot. Since chip cameras have no tube, they have several advantages right away. The first is that the amount of actual electronic circuitry is cut down because the chip is a true low voltage unit. Since the chip requires no high voltage to operate, the entire high voltage circuit has been removed from the camera. This has a two-fold advantage. The obvious one is that less space is needed for circuitry. More important is that the chip camera requires less power to run. Inasmuch as the chip is a solid state unit it has no filament or electron gun. This has cut the amount of heat output of the chip camera by two-thirds over the tube camera. Although it does not seem to be very important, less heat allows the chip camera to be used in a wider variety of situations where ventilation is not readily accessible or possible. Chip cameras also have been able to take

full advantage of the newer "surface mount" and "multi-layered" technology. Although many tube cameras in the late eighties and early nineties used surface mount components (transistors, resisters, etc.) Their size was still dictated by the size and type of tube mounted inside. Therefore they remain somewhat bulky in demeanour. Chip cameras have been able to capture the full potential of surface mount and multi-laired technology cutting their size down to 1/3 or less of their counterparts.

3. Tube cameras have blooming problems. Blooming is the over exaggeration of a bright area or spot within the video picture. This is most evident as a tube shows wear. A beam of electrons is produced in the tube by the electron gun and is propelled at great rates to the front target area of the tube. When an electron makes contact with a point on the photosensitive material of the tube, it causes a discharge. The discharge determines how bright or dark the point of the picture will be. The larger or stronger the discharge, the brighter the point, the less the discharge, the darker. As the cathode of the electron gun in the tube wears out, the electron stream used to discharge the target becomes weaker and weaker. This hampers the tube's ability to fully recover in bright areas of the scene causing a blooming effect. Since the chip has no electron gun or target area, it cannot bloom. Normal wear of the chip will be an overall sensitivity loss causing a general greying of the complete picture.
4. Tube cameras are restricted by general video signal production, as to what enhancements they can have built in. Tubes produce what is known as a linear video signal. To best explain linear, imagine a wave on the ocean going up and down. At the wave's peak it would be white and at its low point it would be black. There would be an infinite amount of gray shades between the top and bottom. This is great for the reproduction of a video image, but has little value for most types of enhancements such

as built-in zoom capabilities, freeze actions, shutter speeds, digital video motion detection, etc. Since the majority of today's enhancements work with digital (computer language) information the tube cameras are greatly hampered requiring outside peripheral equipment to perform most enhancements. This adds bulk and cost to the video system, CCD cameras produce a digital video signal directly from the chip. This allows the manufacturer to perform enhancements in the camera. Cameras are now being designed with built-in-zoom functions saving the cost of expensive zoom lances. They are working with shutter speeds which allow the camera to produce a clear image of very fast moving objects. Some CCD cameras can even be ordered with digital motion detection built in. The amount of possible future enhancements are innumerable and will continue to surface for many years.

5. Tube cameras produce much higher rates of horizontal lines of resolution. For years, the common battle of the chip versus the tube has been the limited number of horizontal lines of resolution that the chip could produce. A tube, depending upon quality and size, can produce as many as 1200 lines of horizontal resolution (typical is between 550 and 650). This has always held the tube camera in high position since it could create such a detailed picture. The limit of the tube comes in its overall picture density. Having a limited grey shade response, tube cameras produced pictures that often appeared soft to the human eye. This is why average person will turn the contrast and brightness on a matter to the maximum output as soon as the video technician leaves the site. CCD cameras on the other hand have a limited availability of horizontal lines of resolution, compensated by a very high density or contrast output. All common chips on the market today average between 400 and 500 actual lines of horizontal resolution and yet because of their

high contrast between white and black, the average person will choose the chip picture over the tube produced the picture. The clarity of the picture is what counts with the chip. If extreme detail is needed for reproduction in the video picture the tube is still the stronger choice of camera.

6. Sensitivity is one point where the tube is still running ahead of chips (as of today). This in part, is due to the type of material that the tube target is made of and also because of the actual construction of the chip. What this relates to in the video system is that serious considerations need to be taken when choosing a camera for a particular application. Light has always been the deciding factor in which camera should be used where. This is slowly becoming a dead issue. Tubes may have an overall stronger sensitivity than chips but the CCD has an overall larger dynamic response to light. What this means is that where the lower light cameras are required to use auto iris lenses to protect the tube in all variances of light conditions, the chip camera can compensate electronically for a large variance in light. That means that the expenses of an auto iris lens for a camera installed in an office area with large windows can now be waylaid in many situations. The future says that the CCD camera will be able to handle the full swing of light levels from night (poorly lit parking lot) with.5 fc of light, to full day (bright sun) at more than 14000 fc of light. If you imagine stepping out of a dark closet into the bright sun without blinking or losing sight, you can have a stronger approbation of what this development will mean to the CCTV industry. Through the design of newer lenses with larger iris apertures as previously discussed, the issue of the CCD camera, enhancement lighting can be designed into the video system.

7. Tube cameras come in five basic types with little variation within each category. Standard vidicon: designed to work in full,

bright, consistent light, Ultricon and Newvicon : designed to work in lower light levels, require the use of auto iris lenses in all variable lighting conditions. Intensified: designed to work in low light levels, require auto iris lenses all the time. Intensified: designed to work in star light. The amount of confusion that has surrounded these cameras over the years regarding proper application has been great. If a standard vidicon camera was installed outside, it could be counted on that the tube would fail within days or months depending upon the amount of actual light. Too many times, lower light cameras were installed inside with auto iris lenses where the light was consistent. Although this didn't create any problems in the life of the camera or the actual production of picture, it was extremely costly. Intensified cameras are far too often installed in well-lit parking areas or equally lighted areas. This has always been a gross error and has resulted in absurd expense due to poor design by individuals who didn't know their trade. To further emphasize the cost factor, it should be known that standard vidicon cameras average between $250.00 and $400.00. Ultricon and Newvicon cameras range between $700.00 and $3000.00. Intensified cameras range between $10000.00 and $ 18000.00.

Intensified/intensified cameras start at $25000.00 and work up very fast. These prices are based on average and user rates without lenses attached. With the mass production of the CCD camera and the further development of the chip itself, several confusing factors have been narrowed down. First the various types of chips are as confined as the tubes are, but the attributes that are available through enhancement capabilities are becoming innumerable. As there are five basic types of tubes, there are three (most common) basic types of CCD sensors. They are CMOS (complementary metal oxide semiconductors), Interline Transfer, and Frame Transfer. Each of these categories of chip has basic advantages for use, as do the tubes, but in a different manner. While the various tube categories dictate the amount of light levels that the camera will produce a favourable picture in, the different CCD categories dictate what the result of different light types will produce in picture. The true test of a chip camera is in what the manufacturer designs around it. There are, however certain basic characteristics will be discussed in detail in the next paragraph. The main point of this comparison of the tube and chip is that the chip camera is considerably more forgiving then the tube camera in later variety of circumstances. This means that one chip camera can handle a wider variety of situations and so will save on many costly mistakes. The eventual advantage is that there will be cameras that will work in all circumstances without high cost or multiple models.

CCD CHIP DEFINITIONS AND DESCRIPTIONS

CMOS (Metal Oxide Semiconductor)

This is least expensive of all the chips to reproduce. It is also the forerunner of the CCD device. It has inherent advantages and disadvantages.

The advantages are:

(a) **Low Cost:** Keeps the overall production costs down.

(b) **High sensitivity to IR:** Gives this chip the ability to work with IR lighting enhancements.

The disadvantages are:

(a) High sensitivity to IR does not make it a desirable chip to be used outside in the bright hot sun.

(b) **Pixel over pixel picture production:** Imagine a room of people sitting at table in neat rows. Each row is 525 people wide and 425 people deep. Each person has a light matter and takes a reading at their location. They must report their reading to central source so that an exact reproduction of the room can be made based upon individual light readings. To report your finding, you and all your counterparts must turn around and climb over each of the tables behind you until you reach the back, at which time your lime of 525 people are marched out to report. Each line of people represents one line of horizontal resolution. This method of picture reproduction is as clumpy as it sounds and so limits the manufacturer's ability to enhance the cameras picture.

(c) **Low sensitivity to low light conditions:** Cmos chip camera has a low sensitivity to low light. This means they require more light to operate than is readily available in a well-lit parking lot. (Average camera sensitivity will vary with manufacturer's enhancements). This camera is best used inside where lighting can remain stronger than outside levels.

(d) **"Fish bone" or grid lines in low light pictures:** when the available light levels drop below an acceptable amount to this camera, a grid like set of white lines may appear in the centre of the picture.

Interline Transfer

This chip was developed in such a way as to improve the picture transfer capabilities of the Cmos chip. In between each vertical row of pixels a vertical shift register was installed. The improved technology also included a new material for the pixels adding to the sensitivity of the chip to lower light levels.

The advantages are:

(a) **Good lower light sensitivity.** Although this is not a low light camera, it can be used in most applications where a 2/3 Ultricon or Newvicon camera can. Within enhancement lighting, or white light enhancement lighting, this camera will work well in all lower light applications.

(b) **Enhanced pixel decoding:** let's return to the room of people as described in point 2 of the Cmos chip. Instead of sitting the people at tables, we will use individual rows of chairs. Between each rows of chairs there is enough room for persons to walk comfortably. Aftcr all persons have taken their light readings, a computer instructs all the people in the odd numbered rows to stand and take a step to their left. They are now in their virtual shift register. They will now proceed in an orderly fashion to the back of the room. As each row reaches the back of the room, they take a sharp right turn and proceed to the main reporting room in the single lines. When all the odd rows have exited, the computer gives the OK to the even numbered rows and the process repeats itself.

(c) **High IR lighting response:** this chip is known for its high sensitivity to IR lighting, making it an excellent choice for IR enhancement lighting.

The disadvantages are:

(a) **Lack of low light sensitivity:** although this chip has lower light sensitivity, it does not easily see in low light areas. This lack of sensitivity is primarily due to the reduced size of the light-sensing pixels and the basic material that they are made of. The pixels are smaller than that of the Cmos chip to allow room for the 500 plus vertical shift registers between each row of pixels.

(b) **IR light sensitivity:** although an advantage in specific circumstances, this chip is sensitive to IR light in the 1200 nanometre scale. Because of this, these cameras come with a field removable IR cut filter. The choice is between the need and preference for a great day picture or a good night picture. Without the IR cut filter, the IR light spectrum is available to the chip during the day. Since IR reflects differently than white light, green grass or leaves will appear white in the sun light. As black asphalt parking lot heats up, it will turn from black to grey or white. If the area becomes too hot, it is possible for the entire picture to go white. If the filter is installed, the day picture will be colour correct, but the night picture will suffer.

An IR cut filter can decrease the available light to the chip by as much as forty percent. This will mean that the night sensitivity will be decreased.

(c) **Smear:** Smear is caused by the overloading of a pixel of light. This happens when the camera views a hot spot or pin point lighting. Pin point lighting may be headlight on a car at night. When one or more pixels overload, the entire row of pixels shuts down. This promotes a fixed vertical white line above and below the point of hot light. Installation of the pop out IR cut filter reduces or removes smear problems. Smear is an inherent problem of chip camera in general.

Frame Transfer

This chip was developed in response to the problems of the interline transfer chip with IR response levels, smear and low light sensitivity. By removing the vertical shift register, in the chips, the individual pixels were able to be increased in size adding to the amount of light sensitive surface exposed to the scene. This action incorporated with the use of different more sensitive photosensitive material, decreased the amount of light needed to produce a good video picture. This new material is less sensitive to IR light, removing the need for IR cut filter and dismissing smear almost completely.

The advantages are:

(a) **A good IR sensitivity for enhancement lighting:** although the IR sensitivity of this style of chip has been reduced far below that of the interline transfer chip. It is still sensitive enough to be used with IR lighting up to the 850/900 nanometre level.

(b) **Less or no smear problems as explained above.** This chip is made with a different photosensitive material and the vertical shift registers have been removed, these are the same culprits that cause smear in the interline transfer chip. Although smear is a basic inherent problem caused by the varying design of the chip, with this combination it is greatly reduced.

(c) **Lower lights sensitivity:** This chip coupled with good electronic enhancements within the camera has reached sensitivity levels equal to the 1" tube camera.

(d) **Complete frame information transfer:** Picture again the rows upon rows of people with individual light meter reading, which need to be processed to the central computer for reproduction. This chip, as it is name states, transfers all rows simultaneously like pulling a lever and dropping the flow out from under the people. Each person falls into a slot just for them and is processed at the leisure of the computer.

Common Rules of Thumb

1. No tube style cameras, and the majority of chip cameras regardless of type, characteristics, cost of lens, filters or location, will produce a favourable picture when looking at an object with bright background.

Typical problem of this type:

Watching a door outside to identify people entering the building: if the cameras are aimed directly at the door the person entering will appear as a silhouette. If the camera is standard vision or has weak Ultricon or Newvicon tube, the picture will wash out and the tube life will be cut in half or more from abuse.

Potential solution:

Aim the camera from the side or facing towards the inside of the area. Increase the interior light with the use of spot lights and / or IR enhancement lighting. Use a properly designed chip camera with a back lit option.

There are a few CCD cameras in the market today with a back lit option. This option gives the camera the ability to electronically enhance the foreground and ignore the background lighting. This will produce a picture where the person in the doorway would be visible and identifiable while the background would appear washed out or extremely bright.

2. Standar vision tube type cameras cannot be used outside under any circumstances even if equipped with, and able to operate an auto iris lens.
3. Standard Vidicon tube, tube type and Cmos chip cameras require full constant light to operate properly and at full capacity.
4. Except under extremely low light condition, SIT, ISIT, or ICCD cameras are not needed for parking lot surveillance.
5. Both hot and cold temperatures need to be considered when choosing a location for any camera.

In the cold weather, 0-f degrees and up, the major concern is the lens. Since it is a mechanical device with grease this unit will stiffen or lock up at temperatures below 35-f degree, causing damage to the lens. The cameras, for the most part, produce enough heat to protect themselves. Temperatures below 0-f will require that heat is provided for the camera.

Heat is a problem to the camera. Overheated situations, above 115-f, will cause failure of many circuits within the camera. This will produce video pictures with various degrees of horizontal disruption or it may cause the camera to shut down completely.

Possible Solution

Install heaters in all camera housing where the temperature could drop below 35-f degrees. Buy housings where the concentrated heat is in front for the lens. Install blowers in all housing that will be installed in areas where the potential heat could rise above 75-f degrees. Blowers keep the interior air moving allowing the heat to more evenly dissipate through the material of the housing cover; keep in mind that all cameras produce heat. This is important in the summer heat, since the camera's own heat will add to the effect of the outside temperature. All housings that are installed in the sun should, at all times, have sun shields installed. These shields are nothing more than a metal cover that sits about an inch or two above the housing. The sun hits the shield and the natural movement of air between the shield and housing dissipates the heat from the shield saving the camera inside the housing from damage.

6. Ultricon, Newvicon, SIT, ISIT and most CCD cameras require auto iris lenses in applications of variable light.
7. IR cut filters will cut back the available light to the tube of CCD by as much as 25%. Though not a problem in the day, this could prove to be a major problem at night when light is most scarce.
8. Tube type and CCD chip cameras cannot view bright areas and dark areas simultaneously. See point #1 options.

Cameras equipped with a peak average adjustment have the ability to be adjusted in the field for best picture of either the dark area or the bright area. The scene must be 2/3 bright with 1/3 dark or 2/3 dark with 1/3 bright. This is because of the camera's design. If the area to be viewed is ½ bright and ½ dark, the peak average adjust will not work.

9. The more sensitive the tube or chip, the more expensive it will be to re-tube/re-chip.
10. The more sensitive the tube, the less tube life is expected.

Lens Considerations and Choices

When choosing a lens to perform in a CCTV site, there are several considerations that must be taken before the actual decision is made. Although choosing a lens is a fairly simple procedure, it is probably the second most important design of the entire job (the first being type of camera) unfortunately, too many sales people, installers and end users know little or nothing about how to properly choose the best lens for the job.

The first decision must be to determine the actual area to be viewed at the monitor point.

1. Does a wide area at short range need to be viewed? If so, a wide angle lens is needed.
2. Does an average scene at medium distances need to be viewed? If so, a standard lens is needed.
3. Does a narrow area at a long range need to be viewed? If so, a telephoto lens is needed.
4. Does an area representing question 1 and 2 and 3 needs to be viewed? If so, a zoom lens is needed.

The easiest method to determine the answers to the above questions is the "T" method. First picture the letter T lying on its side. The stem of the T will equal the distance from the camera to the subject being viewed. The crossbar of the T will equal the total picture or scene to be viewed. If only one T is needed, a slandered, fixed focal length lens will work fine. If two or more Ts are needed, a zoom lens is needed. (See diagram)

The second step is to decide the type of camera that will be used.

1. Is the camera a standard Vidicon? If so, a fixed iris lens is needed.
2. Is the camera an Ultricon, Newvicon, CCD, SIT, or ICCD? If so, an auto iris lens is needed.
3. Is the camera a 1/3", ½", 2/3" or a 1" format? A 2/3" formatted lens is needed for a 2/3" camera, a 1" formatted lens can be used on any format camera.

Note: a larger formatted lens will always work on a smaller formatted camera; however a smaller formatted lens cannot be used on larger formatted cameras.

4. Is the camera a colour one? If so, a lens designed for colour is needed.

Once the above question is answered a few simple calculations can be made on paper and the proper lens for the proper job can be ordered.

Focal Length

To determine the size or focal length of lens needed for a job, it must first be understood how the size of the lens affects the size of the picture on the monitor. The monitor picture will always be wider than it is high. The height to width ratio of the monitor and the area of view will be constant at different distances. For this reason a paper calculation or lens selection slide rule may be used to pick the right lens with great accuracy.

The focal length (1) of a lens is a measure of the relative magnification. A 1" lens magnifies linear dimensions 1/3 times more than a 2/3" lens at the same camera-to-subject distance.

Focal lengths are measured in millimetre; lenses have been standardized throughout the industry. Standard is the term applied to lens that will produce a picture equivalent to the human eye at the same distance. Since tube and chip size play a major role in the final picture, each standard size of the tube and/or CCD chip (i.e. 1", 2/3") will have different standard lens sizes. The standard lens for each camera size is the starting point for all calculations concerning scene width and height.

The millimetre number rating of a lens will get bigger for telephoto and smaller for wide angle. What this mean is that the smaller the number, the more scene will be viewed both in width and height. Wide angle lenses are generally used for up-close applications where a wide area is needed but a short distance of camera-to-subject is available (i.e. apartment house entrance way by the intercom). Telephoto lenses are generally used for long distance shots where a specific area is to be viewed up close (i.e. parking lot entrances being viewed from a building 200" feet away). Standard lenses are used when the scene to be reproduced for ID purposes is comfortable to the human eye (i.e. bank lobbies and/or office areas where distances remain within 20 to 25 feet). Zoom lenses are used when a multiple of scenes near and far are to be viewed (i.e. parking lots outer parameters of properties).

It should be noted that any time a zoom lens is used in a CCTV system, the lens should never exceed a 10:1 ratio. If the low and or wide angle of the lens is 12.5 mm, the long or telephoto of the zoom lens should not exceed 12.5 mm. This is due primarily to the light loss that occurs when the lens is in the full telephoto position.

Field of View

When dealing with lenses of any size, there is consideration called "FIELD OF VIEW" referring to the actual size of area that will be seen at specific distance using different lenses.

The field of view changes as the length of the lens changes.

Example: A 16mm lens on a 2/3" camera will produce a scene that is 14 feet wide and 10 feet 6" tall, 25 feet from the camera.

A 25mm lens on a 2/3" camera will produce a scene that is 9 feet wide and 7 feet tall, 25 feet from the camera.

When a person refers to the field of view of a lens in relationship to a camera, he/she is referring to the specific size, both wide and tall, of the area being viewed at a specific distance from the camera.

A 1" camera will have a different field of view from a 2/3" camera using the same length lens. This is due to the actual viewing size of the imager.

Example: A 25mm lens on a 1" camera will produce a scene that is 13 feet wide 10 feet, 25 feet from the camera.

A 25mm lens on a 2/3" camera will produce a scene that is 9 feet wide and 7 feet tall, 25 feet from the camera.

The width of the field of view will always be more than the height. This is caused by the scanning field of the tube and/or the CCD chip. The monitor's reproduction of the picture will likewise be wider than tall.

The field of view that a lens will have on a camera at specific distances is determined by a few simple calculations based upon the format size of the imager, both horizontal and vertical, the focal length of the lens to be used, and the distance that the camera will be at from the scene to be viewed.

Depth of Field

Depth of field is a term that relates to what portion of a picture is in focus and what portion of the picture is out of focus at any given light level or iris opening at specific distances.

The wider the angle of the lens, the more depth of field the picture will have. The longer the telephoto capabilities of the lens, the shorter or narrower the depth of field will be.

Example: The depth of field of a 25mm lens focused on any object 25 feet away at full daylight will be 3.2 feet to infinity. Any object closer to the camera than 3.2 feet will be out of focus. All objects beyond 3.2 feet will be in focus.

The depth of field of a 75mm lens focused on an object 25 feet away at full daylight will be 15.8 feet to 59.4 feet. Any object closer to the camera than 15.8 feet will be out of focus. Likewise, any object farther away than 59.4 feet will be in focus.

A common rule of thumb is the shorter the lens length (8mm, 16mm, etc.), the wider the depth of field will be. The longer the lens (25mm, 50 mm, etc.), the shorter or narrower the depth of field will be.

A second rule of thumb applies to light and the speed of the lens. Fast lens is a lens that has a very small f-stop or very large aperture. F-1.4 considered a fast lens; f-8 is considered a slow lens.

The slower the lens and/or the more light available, the wider the depth of field will be. The faster the lens and/or or the less light available the narrower the depth of field will be.

This application could have a great effect on the customers ability to view and entire scene at all times of day or night.

Example: The customer needs to view three objects 24 hours per day. The first object is 15 feet away, the second is 25 feet away, and the third is 50 away. The customer needs to have a field of view of at least ½ feet wide on on the object that is 25 feet away. This forces the customer to have a lens with a focal length of 50mm.

During the day the 50mm lens will have a depth of field of 9.4 feet to infinity, therefore, objects #1, #2, #3 will all be in focus. During the night the 50 mm lens will have a depth of field of 22.6 to 28 feet. The problem here is that objects #1 and #3 will be out of focus while object #2 looks great. The four solutions to the above problem are:

1. Increase the angle of the lens to a 25mm or wider, which will have a broader depth of field
2. Increase the available light at night so that all three objects are enhanced to a twilight type atmosphere.
3. Accept the situation as is during the day and compromise at night.
4. Install a zoom lens allowing multiple fields of view.

Zoom Lenses

The term zoom, in lenses, refers to the ability of the lens to physically alter its view from wide to narrow. In simpler terms, a zoom lens can either make objects that are far away appear near and large, or it can make them appear far away and small.

Zoom lenses come in a large variety of wide-to-far configuration. As with a standard fixed focal length lens, sizes of zoom lenses are referred to in millimetres. The only significant difference is that a zoom lens will have two focal lengths, usually in order of smallest number (widest area) to largest number (longest view).

Example: typical zoom lens is 16mm to 160 mm.

A zoom lens has the ability to have the equivalent focal length of any fixed focal length lens between 166 and 160 millimetres. This wide sweeping arrangement allows the end user to have a multitude of views at the touch of a button.

Zoom lenses are most popular in parking lots and large outside perimeter applications where multiple scenes need to be observed.

Picking a proper zoom lens entails the same formulas and calculations as does any focal length for a standard lens the only difference is that both a near scene and a far scene width and height, must be taken into consideration.

The majority of zoom lenses used with CCTV systems are motor driven. The motor gives the operator the ability to "zoom" in on a distant object to observe with more detail, or, to back off from an object to see more of the surrounding area and actions, for this reason, considerations must be given to the type of control system that will be used in conjunction with the lens.

The most common problem related to zoom lenses is focal tracking. Focal tracking or tracking, is the capability of the lens to maintain the focal integrity of the picture when moving from a full telephoto position to a wide angle position.

If the ratio of the distance between the camera's tube or chip and the aperture of the lens are not of a precise measurement, the lens will not be able to track properly. Consequently the operator would need to constantly focus the picture as he/she moves the scene from a telephoto (long range) picture to a wide angle scene.

Curing a camera/lens with bad or no focal tracking can be accomplished through back-focusing. This a procedure of alignment and can be done in the field.

IRIS and F-Stop Explanation

To totally understand the lens is to understand the iris and its importance to the proper operation of the video camera in relationship to the picture.

The iris is a simple mechanism used to vary the diameter of the aperture; some irises are made of a number of thin shaped metal blades that surround the aperture, each blade having a lower stud at one end and an upper stud at the other end. The lower studs fall into holes in a fixed ring surrounding the aperture, while the upper studs are held by radial slots in a table control ring. Newer style lenses are being developed that have a single shutter style iris, allowing them to be maintenance free.

The aperture of the lens is the final opening through which light is passed through before being focused on the chip or tube.

The purpose of the iris is to adjust the amount of light or scene reflection that is allowed into the camera with a high sensitivity to light (low light camera), to operate in full daylight as well as in low light situations. During a bright period of light the iris should be closed, allowing a small portion of light to pass through. In a dark period the iris should be opened, allowing the full portion of light available to pass through. In a moderate period of light, the iris would be partially closed, allowing a moderate portion of light to pass to the chip or tube.

The size of the opening made by the aperture, or iris, is measured in "f-stops", f-stops are relative to the amount of light allowed to pass through an aperture under controlled circumstances, and so are standardized throughout the lens industry. A lens for a 35mm film camera will have the same f-stop numbers as a lens for a closed circuit camera.

F-stops are numbers; the smaller the number, the larger the opening at the aperture or iris, the larger the number, the smaller the opening or aperture. F-stops will always be measured with the following numbers: f-8, f-1.4, f-2, f-2.8, f-4, f-5.6, f-8, f-11, f-16 and f-22 Each number refers to the reduction of the aperture size by the lens.

IRIS Opening

IRIS Opening with Setting of f-22

IRIS Opening with Setting of f-8

IRIS Opening with Setting of f-1.4

Example: F-22 means that the lens opening is 1/22 as large as the actual aperture opening. It would be used in bright light where only a small amount was needed by a chip or tube.

Each full f-stop down on the lens will decrease the light being focused on the chip or tube by 50%.

A fixed iris is just what it sounds like. It is a lens with an aperture of a specific size built in with no ability to be adjusted manually or automatically. A setting of

f-1.4 would be used on a standard video when it needs as much light as possible to operate.

A manual iris lens is a lens that is designed to have an iris that will remain in one position until it is manually altered by turning a ring on the outside of the lens.

A common misconception about auto-iris lenses that are controlled by the camera is that the lens takes commands directly from the camera, dictating when to open or close the iris. Consequently, whenever there are picture problems in a video system caused by the iris being open too much or too little, the lens is the first place where the finger of blame is pointed. In actuality, over fifty percent (50%) of problems related to iris operation turn out to be camera problems related to the actual video signal being produced.

Video signals being emitted by the camera will change in amplitude (size) according to the amount of light of the scene being focused on the chip or tube. The more light being focused on the chip or tube, the larger the video signal that will be emitted from the camera, the lesser the light, the smaller the video signal from the camera.

Consequently, as the video sampling system of the lens, or lens controller, senses increase in the amplitude (size) of the video signal (being produced by the camera) that go beyond a preset (field adjustable) size, due to increase in scene lighting, it will command the iris to close. This action of closing the iris will cut down the light passing through the lens onto the chip or tube and cause the video signal to decrease indirect proportion until it fits into the preset calculations of the video sampling system, at which time the iris will stop and remain in a fixed position until it is again commanded to open or close.

If the light decreases, as in the example of day turning into night, the signal will decrease proportionately, as the video signal gets smaller than the preset boundaries of the video sampling system of the lens, this system will command the iris to open. Eventually, in night or dark situation, the lens iris will be open to its full potential allowing the maximum light available to pass through the lens onto the chip or tube.

Lighting and Its Effects

Because light affects everything from picture clarity to focus, it is essential that you understand what is happening.

Light in use with video is measured in several terms, eacha little more confusing than the first. The three most common units of measure in video are foot-candles, lux and foot lamberts. Each of these light measuring names is related to the other and can be cross calculated to fit each other's terms.

To make things simpler, the definitions given below can be applied to each measurement.

Footcandle (fc): The amount of light as measured in an area of one square foot when the light source is uniform and equal in brightness, and coming from a source that is equal in distance at all points from the point of measure, and is one lumen in brightness.

Lux: The metric conversion of foot-candles. One lux =.0929 fc.

Footlambert (fL): A unit of light equal to 1/3.1416 foot-candle.

For simplicity, the footcandles will be used as reference in this workbook.

Under normal circumstances the lighting of a scene outside will not come into consideration during the day. Daylight will range from 10 to 1,000 footcandles typically on an overcast day, and from

1,000 to 14,000 on a sunny day. These conditions will be handled with ease by any Ultricon. Newvicon, SIT, or ISIT tube or chip type cameras equipped with a proper auto iris lens as recommended by the manufacturer.

Interior lighting, on the other hand, can cause problems. Although a scene may have constant light applied at all times, that light may not be enough for standard Vidicon type cameras to work under properly. At this point a more sensitive type of camera may be needed. The use or need for an auto iris lens, on a lower light camera, may be optional, dependent, upon the consistency of the light affecting the scene.

Example: If in a warehouse with poor lighting, the average illumination of an area is as little as 10 footcandles, this would not be enough for a standard Vidicon camera to operate properly. If the warehouse had no windows, doors, or other type of opening to the outside, the light will remain extremely constant. This situation would constitute the use of a manual iris lens. The lens opening could be set manually, based on video signal size. If in this warehouse, there were doors, windows, or other type openings that allowed light from another unstable store, an auto iris would be necessary to compensate for the fluctuating light source.

Interior lighting can be easily calculated by using a light meter at the scene to be monitored. Light meters do just as their name indicates; they measure the available light at a point. Light meters can be purchased at any local camera store.

If it is not possible, or is inconvenient, to be on site to measure light, a simple tool called a lens selector calculator can be used. These simple slide rule calculators are available at any of the large manufacturers or their representatives. The cost of this calculator will range from nothing to a couple of dollars.

A complex looking tool, the lens selector calculator can be used and mastered by anyone was can read numbers quickly and easily.

These calculators will determine the focal length of a lens needed for a specific scene and/or camera (including room lenses), f-stop or aperture opening necessary for proper illumination of scene, and usually they will also have an illumination guide that will help determine how much light is available under most circumstances through simple descriptions. They will also tell you the depth of field of a scene at varying light scales and f-stops.

Outside lighting can be the most treacherous to any camera system. Because of the extreme light difference between night and day, the depth of field of the lens will vary dramatically.

Depth of field, in simplest terms, is the amount of area before and after the centre of view that will be in relatively good focus. This is due to the amount, of light available and the light refraction capabilities of the lens in proportion to the size of the aperture.

Example: During day, or full light, the depth of field is very deep, both near and far. What this means is that a car in the background, at fifty feet will be in good focus even though the actual object being observed in the scene is at thirty feet.

At night the depth of field becomes very shallow, both near and far. What this means is that a car, in the background at fifty feet will probably be indistinguishable if the actual object being observed in the scene is at thirty feet.

Because of this characteristic of light's relationship to the depth of field, a camera with a great day picture may have a night picture that is so out of focus that it appears to be absent, even one has adjusted the focus.

2X Tele-Converters

A common tool used in the field of lenses is the 2X tele-converters. This small lens gives the user the ability to double the actual working size of the lens installed. For example, a 12.5 mm lens with a 2X tele-converter attached will become a 25mm lens.

One of the three major drawbacks of a 2X tele-converter is that the available light in the scene to the imager is cut by as much as 50% or one full f-stop, reducing the camera's ability to work under most circumstances by that much or more.

The second drawback is that the clarity of the overall picture is degraded by as much as 40%, causing problems related to picture identification and to overall customer satisfaction.

The third major drawback is that the camera loses all possible capabilities of proper local tracking when using the 2X tele-converter with a room lens. The customer will either have access to focus on something very far or very near, but not both.

It is recommended that in those situations where a customer is trying to use a 2X tele-converter lens, he/she be steered away from it, with suggestions to add another camera locations, and/or drop the idea completely.

Coaxial Cable

An old man once said that the penny saved in construction often costs a dollar in the rebuild. What this translates into as far as coaxial cable is concerned is that it does not pay to buy a cheap cable to do the job. Good coaxial is not cheap; cheap coaxial is the largest cause of problems related to new and old closed circuit video systems.

Although there are a varieties of coaxial cables available for use with the CCTV system there are only a few that are reliable. The major factors to keep in mind when choosing a coaxial cable for use in a system, are broken down into five categories.

Category 1. Environmental Conditions: As is to be expected when choosing a coaxial cable the first consideration must be given to the jacket of the cable. At no time can an indoor cable be used outside or in burial conditions. The video signal will be lost to co-ground faults and corrosion. Picking the proper cable is as easy as reading the specifications listed on the reel or asking the cable supplier to recommend the proper jacket material for the job.

Category 2. Shielding: Although shielding comes in a variety of types, it is relatively easy to choose a proper one, rule number one is to avoid aluminium whenever possible, although first wrapped dielectrics will operate under good conditions, aluminium shields do not provide a good attenuations of the video signal over great lengths. The best possible shield available is copper braid. This type of shield will carry the proper signal with little or no interference for the looping distances.

If running the coaxial cable through a high induction field (generator rooms, long runs parallel to high voltage, etc) it may be required to have a double shield or triaxial cable. This type of cable has two separate shields protected from each other by an insulator of some type. The outer shield will be attached to a good earth ground at one of the cables, allowing all RF interference to be drained to the ground without affecting the video signal.

Getegory 3. Dielectric: Dielectrics come in a number of types and materials. The dielectric tunes the coaxial cable for a 75-ohm impedance. If a cable with any other impedance is in the system, it will not carry the harmonics of the video signal properly and will cause various symptoms ranging from ghost figures to noisy or poor quality pictures at the monitor.

Category 4. Centre Core: The second most important factor of any coaxial cable is the type of centre core being used to carry the video signal. One hundred percent copper will always be the best choice for CCTV systems. Copper coated, tin centre cores carry a good video signal, but do not hold up under long distances and/or bad weather conditions. All that means is that a re-cable job may be necessary after a couple of years, if copper–coated tin is used outside. Aluminium centre cores cannot be used with closed circuit video systems under any condition. Even short runs can introduce harmonics into the system. Harmonics are unwanted frequencies that distort and deteriorate video signals.

The second consideration of the centre core is the type of wire used. It will either be a single solid wire (slid) or several small stranded wires twisted together (flex). If the job site consists of several stationary mounted cameras, then solid coaxial cable is a fine choice. If, however, the site consists of cameras mounted on pan and or pan / tilt units, the flex cable should be considered at the site of the camera and pan / tilt unit and or any other location where the cable may flex. Solid cable is not designed to move and will break internally in the coaxial cable.

It should be noted at this point that solid core and stranded cables may be used together within the same system. The major runs within the systems can be installed using solid core cable to save money. At the points where pan/tilt or pan units are used, stranded cables can be installed as a patch to the unit.

Category 5. Cable Size: A very important decision that must be made at the design point of any systems is- what is the distance of each cable run from the camera to the monitor point? Distance determines cable size. Coaxial cables used with closed circuit video systems come in three sizes that are most common.

RG-59-A short run cable with average acceptable runs of up to 1000

RG-6-A medium run cable with average acceptable runs of up to 1500

RG-II-A long distance cable with average acceptable runs of up to 3000

Obviously, the length of the acceptable cable run will be dependent on factors such as RF field, type of shield, centre core, and dielectric. If using the best cable possible at the onset (100% copper centre core with 100% braided copper shield), the above distances will be easily achieved. If using a lesser coaxial cable (copper-coated tin centre core, aluminium foil shield) then it must be calculated to receive as much as 25% less distance to receive the same quality video signal at the monitoring point.

All coaxial cables used in industrial closed circuit video must be rated at 75 ohms of impedance (AC resistance), regardless of the type of shield, centre core, or jacket.

The reasons for this statement are simple:

1. All industrial closed circuit cameras regardless of type of manufacture, are designed to unit a video signal that is balanced at 75 ohm impedance.
2. All monitors, switches time lapse recorders, amplifiers, ground loop correctors, etc. are designed to receive a balanced composite video signal at 75 ohm impedance.

Non-Coaxial Transmission

If more distance is required than the coaxial cable is rated for, then video line amplifiers, optic transmissions, microwave transmissions, telephone line transmissions, and/or laser transmissions systems may be more cost-effective and/or more easily installed for quality needed.

Systems that have long distance cable runs, heavy interference from electrical fields, either man made or natural (lightning), strong potential for ground faults, and/or have major aerial cable runs outside, are prime candidates for other forms of video transmission.

The composite video signal emitted by the camera is only 1 to 12 volts peak to peak, with less push than a drop of water rolling down a hot, dry sidewalk. One AAA battery used in a calculator has more power than a good composite video signal. Understanding this, it is easy to comprehend why so much value is placed on the method and/or type of signal carrier that is to be used in any video system. Coaxial cable, although the least expensive of all types available, is limited to distance, surrounding conditions, and a multiple other obstacles, for this reason it is not always the wisest choice of video transmitters.

A few of the stronger choice for video transmission are listed below.

Microwave

Microwave transmission is the sending of the video signal from point to point without cable interconnection. This is accomplished by converting the video signal to an AM or FM radio signal at the camera and converting the signal back to video at the monitor.

Advantages of the microwave system:

1. Covers large distance without cabling.
2. Works on a broad frequency bandwidth, allowing for very good picture reproduction.
3. Eliminates long cable runs etc.
4. Additional costs and other labour costs may be offset by the savings of not cabling.

Disadvantages of the microwave system:

1. Must be a line of sight transmission.
2. Requires FCC licensing.
3. Fog, flocks of birds and/or insects, heavy rains, heavy snows, and other physical interferences can restrict the signal partially and/or completely, causing poor picture quality from time to time.
4. High costs up front.

Infrared Laser

The infrared laser system converts the video signal into a modulated beam of light, shooting it through the air from the transmitter to the receiver. As with the microwave system the laser requires both receiver and transmitter.

Advantages of infrared laser:

1. Able to transmit over long distances.
2. Unaffected by electrical or radio frequency disturbances.
3. No licensing required.
4. Easily relocated and realigned (good for temporary installations).
5. No cabling required (between transmission point and receiver).

6. Works on a broad frequency band width allowing for good picture quality.

Disadvantages of Infrared laser:

1. Extra costs involved for transmission and receiving stations.
2. Must be a line of sight between transmitter and receiver.
3. Must be mounted on a very solid platform or wall (no vibration).
4. Fog, heavy rain, heavy snow, flocks of birds, and/or insects can interfere with picture
5. Shooting over large areas that reflect sun's heat will cause the laser to bend and affect the picture dramatically (i.e. large parking lots, sand beaches, roads etc).

Slow Scan Systems

The slow scan system converts the video signal into digital pulses that are sent one frame at a time over standard telephone company lines. Since the system is only able to transfer one frame at a time, the process is very slow and much of the action is lost between update information transmissions. The slow scan system requires the installation of a transmitter in the camera and a receiver to convert the digital pulses back to video at the monitor.

Advantages of the slow scan system:

1. Able to transmit video signals anywhere in the world from the source via standard telephone company systems.

Disadvantages of the slow scan system:

1. Up-front costs of the transmitter and receiver.
2. Narrow frequency bandwidth causing low resolution of the picture.
3. Able to transmit only on frame of video information at a time causing loss of information.

Fibre Optics

Fibre optic transmission is the second most popular type of video transmission and is fast becoming the trend. When fibre optics is used in a video system, the electrical video signal from the camera or controller is translated into a pulse of light that is injected into a fine (size of a hair) piece of glass or plastic cable. This light travels the length of the cable to a receiver at the other end, where the light is turned back into an electrical video signal.

Because light is used as the carrier, the video and/or control signals are no longer susceptible to outside interferences such as radio frequency (rf), inducted electrical pulses from high voltages, lightning, data ground faults (gf) or a multitude of other interfering electromagnetic forces that can play havoc with the video signal and/or destroy video equipment when transmitted via coaxial cable.

Jacket: Jacket the outside of the cable is referred to as the jacket. The jacket can be made up of several different types of material, depending upon the need. In air plenums, a jacket made up of Teflon is needed to prevent noxious gases from being produced in the event of a fire. Underground or outdoor applications require a jacket that will not rot or break down from natural forces.

It should be noted at this point that fibre optic cable has an expected field life of 35 years, whereas coaxial cable has an expected life of only of only 20 years.

Shield and Case: Under the jacket of the fibre optic cable is a shield made up of fibrous threads woven together to enhance the strength of the overall cable. Below the shield is the case of the cable. The case is most often tubular in design. It is made up of a plastic or pressed paper material, and is used to provide some rigidity to the cable to prevent the internal fibre from being bent or broken.

Optic Carrier: The final section of the fibre optic cable is the optic carrier. The optic carrier is made of either plastic or glass, and will be thinly coated with a material designed to give it strength.

The most common type of fibre optic carrier used in video today is constructed of glass and is 50 microns in diameter.

There is much work being done in the field of fibre optics today ad many new developments are being brought to the surface regularly, some companies have had limited success with 100 and 200 micron cables to carry their video signals. However the 100 and 200 micron cables are considered outdated and clumsy. The 50 and 62-1/2 microns cables are the accepted standards in the industry and are also the least expensive cable available.

Because the video signal is translated into light and injected into the fibre, much greater distance of cable can be used in comparison to its counterpart, coaxial cable, depending on the type of transmitter and receiver used and the type of fibre optic carrier, the video signal can be transmitted anywhere from one foot to five miles without need of amplification.

For many years fibre optic transmission of video signals was restricted to a single video image transmitted in a single direction per fibre. This limited the use of fibre in many systems using data control signals that travelled with the video signals via the coaxial cable. Today it is possible to transmit up to four real time video signals or two-way videos and two -way data signals on a single fibre. The cost savings of this method over that of hardwire or multiple coaxial cables can be significant.

Balancing Costs with Quality

The major deterrent to using fibre optics today is the cost and labour involved. Fifty micron cables will cost between 10 and 15 percent more per foot than a high quality coaxial such as the BELDON RG9250. This cost-per-foot disadvantage quickly disappears, however, when savings on service labour due to lightning, ground faults, electrical interferences, and a multitude of other problems that arise when using coaxial begin to mount up.

If put into perspective, ground fault connectors, lightning/surge protectors, in-line voice amplifiers, and other such enhancement equipment needed for coaxial jobs drive the cost of a video system up very quickly.

The fibre optic connectors are expensive. Because this is a different form of cable than the average company is accustomed to working with, the thought of spending $500 to $1,500 for a connector polishing tool kit and line verification meters is a major turnoff, not to mention the initial training needed to make connections.

All forms of electronics require a certain amount of investment in proper tools and training. The expense of a connector kit and cable test meter is a one-time out-of-pocket investment that will allow the company making the expenditure to move into the future and cut its overall video expenses considerably.

Advantages of Fibre Optics:

1. Able to transmit over long distances without amplification.
2. Broad frequency bandwidth allowing for very good video resolution.
3. Cannot transmit or carry electrical or radio interferences regardless of how strong the field is around the cable.
4. Eliminates ground faults, loops.
5. Extremely reliable source of transmission.
6. Able to transmit multiple bi-directional signals within a single cable.
7. Unaffected by electrical storms.
8. Smaller more pliable cable than coaxial cables.

Disadvantages of Fibre Optics:

1. Expensive cable (10 % to 15% more than coaxial).
2. One-time expense for test and installation equipment.
3. Training necessary for connection points.
4. **Cannot be used in radioactive environments.**

Application and Size

The single most common misconception about monitors is that they are overpriced black and white televisions. End users often ask what the purpose of a monitor is and why they can't watch television programs on their video system.

To compare a monitor to a black and white (or colour) television is like comparing apples to oranges. The average television is designed to operate for a five year period, base upon the average of 8 hours a day per unit. This equals a total of 14,600 hours of use in its lifetime. The monitor is designed to continuously work for 24 hours per day for an average 5 year period. This equals a total of 43,800 tours of use in its lifetime.

A television is designed to work on VHF (very high frequencies) and UHF (ultra high frequencies) being transmitted through the air. The monitor is designed to work with composite video signals being transmitted via a balanced cable.

The average television has 525 TVL (Typical Vertical Lines) of resolution, while the video monitor has 525 TVL and from 600 to 1200 THL.

In short the monitor is designed to work with the industrial closed circuit video system and will outlast, and outperform, the consumer television at an overall lesser cost.

Monitors are available in a variety of sizes. Choosing the proper size for the proper application is a relatively easy process if two simple rules are remembered.

1. The distance between the monitor and the viewer will have a direct effect upon the clarity of the picture as seen by the viewer. The closer the operator is to the monitor, the smaller the screen should be; and the farther away the operator is from the monitor the larger the screen should be to maintain proper resolution.
2. A monitor with 700 or more lines of resolution will produce a picture in direct proportion to the number of lines of resolution

transmitted to it. In simpler terms, a 700 line monitor will produce 700 lines even if a 1000 lines camera is used. This does not mean that a 700 line monitor will make a better picture out of a 300 line camera transmission; the monitor in this case would spread out the available picture causing a slight degrading of the picture produced by the camera.

The size of a monitor is determined by the size of the viewing area of the screen as measured from bottom left corner to top right corner, to properly determine what size monitor is needed for a particular application, the following formula can be used.

Monitor size in inches–4 = most comfortable viewing distance in feet +/- 25%.

Example

9” Monitor–4 = 5 feet screen to viewer for best picture +/–1.25ft.

12” Monitor–4 = 8 feet screen to viewer for best picture +/– 2.00ft.

Location and Layout

A second misconception in the CCTV industry is that the more monitors installed in a single viewing room, the more an operator can watch.

There have been several studies into the number of monitors, the angle of the monitor to the operator and the total effective time of viewing that an operator can work with.

The final recommendation boils down to a few solid points that must be taken into consideration during the design of the viewing room of the system.

1. The angel from which a monitor is viewed becomes less effective for each 5 degrees it is rotated from centre. In other words, design the console or viewing area in such a way that the monitor to be viewed by the operator is aimed straight on

from wherever the operator is sitting. A monitor that is installed so that the viewing surface of the monitor is at an angle of 45 degrees or more away from the operator, cannot be viewed properly and will lose as much as 50% of its effective purpose as a line of sight detection.

2. A perfect system will have only one monitor to be viewed at any time. The maximum number of monitors to be viewed by a single operator should never exceed four. A good arrangement of monitors will have one master monitor. Usually 15 inch, and to four secondary smaller monitors, usually 9 inch.

Since angles have already been established as a factor, the position and angle of the main monitor should be centred to the operator with no angle to the view. The four secondary monitors should be located either on each side of the master in pairs, or all four on a single side. The angle of the secondary monitors should be designed to slant or tilt toward to operator.

In the system where an extreme number of cameras do not permit the use of only four monitors, such peripherals as the quad splitter, multiplexed splitter, or video switches with alarm input capability may be used.

Operator Fatigue

Throughout the entire monitor section of this book, I have been referring to the angle of the monitors, size, position in relation to viewing, and the amount of time that an operator can and does stay effective while viewing the closed circuit video system.

Time is the single most neglected factor in the design of most closed circuit video systems. By the time I am referring to the overall effect that watching an angle and/or multiple monitors has on an operator after a specific amount of time. The longer an operator watches a monitor the less he/she sees.

After approximately one hour (less time for below average

intelligence) the operator's mind has shut off the monitor to the point that an object can be moved into and consequently through the scene at a rate of 6 inches per minute. Although this may not sound like a lot of motion, the overall effect on a field of view that is twelve feet wide would be to completely pass through it in a matter of twenty four minutes. A lot of merchandise can be stolen at this rate.

In the above case would the observer be at fault, or would the system be at fault?

On some high security military and government sites, the video operators and observers are rotated between posts as often as every hour. This keeps the operator completely fresh at all times, obviously, the average closed circuit video system owner is not going to hire and train enough observers to rotate them each hour, but, he/she should be made aware during the design of the system to work with everything at his/her disposal to ensure a quality run program as well as a quality designed and installed system.

A second key factor to the link of time and video monitoring is operator's IQ. It has been proven that the higher the operators IQ. The longer it takes for a system to become dull and routine. When dealing with a lower IQ level person, it will be necessary to shift posts and responsibility more often to obtain and maintain the same standards of security video monitoring.

The last word is:

The higher the security risk being monitored by an observer,

- the more complex the alarm interface to the video system should be,
- the fewer monitors should be used to observe,
- the higher the IQ of the average operator should be, and
- the more often the operators should be rotated between posts.

Eight-Step Analysis

Choosing the right video switches for a job is a simple process, but there are a few steps involved to determine which switches will be the best for each job.

1. How many cameras will be switched on at each monitor point? Monitor point is the area where the video picture will be viewed.
2. Will any of the cameras within the video system be viewed at more than one monitor point, and if yes, will the individual monitor points need separate controlling capabilities? Controlling capabilities refer to pulling up individual pictures and/or controlling lenses and/or pan/tilt units.
3. Will there be any interface alarm trigger points?
4. Will there be one, two, or more monitors connected to the same switcher?
5. Will it be necessary to have individual switching or dwell times between cameras?
6. Will the switcher be required to trip any other devices such as recorders, buzzers, lights, etc in the event of an alarm?
7. Are there plans to expand this system in the future, and if yes, will there be room on this switching system to handle the expansion?
8. Will this unit need to be rack mounted or table top?

The final choice of a video switcher will not be made until the majority of the video system is already in place, on paper. Only at that point can the proper unit be chosen. We will trace each question out completely, looking for the necessary information to make a proper choice.

How many cameras will be switched at each monitor point?

Since most video switchers come with an even number of camera inputs, this question is more dependent upon growth and expansion of the video system. For instance, a new system has three cameras, the nearest video switcher available without special order will have four camera inputs, if the customer is planning to expand his/her system to six cameras within the next two years, the only consideration would be the upfront cost of a six or eight position video switcher. If there were no plans for expansion of the video system, a four input video switcher will suffice.

Will any of the cameras within the video system be viewed at more than one monitor point, and if yes, will the individual monitor points need separate controlling capabilities?

The sole purpose of this question is to determine if a secondary monitor point could or should be handled by a loop through, or, bridging switcher. A loop through monitor gives the user the ability to pass the video from a camera through the first video switcher to a secondary point, second monitor, second switching point, etc without affecting the video signal, if the loop through switcher loses power for any reason, the video would still pass through it to the secondary point. A bridging switcher does not pass the video from each camera through it directly, but rather has a secondary monitor output. This secondary monitor output is almost always locked onto a single camera at all times and is controlled by the operator at the switcher location. If power is removed from the bridging switcher, video pictures would be lost at both monitor points. If it is deemed necessary to have multiple monitor points, a single switcher may be ordered as a looping, bridging switcher. This switcher gives the ability to pass the video from a camera directly through the primary switching point to a secondary point, while providing one switching and one fixed monitor point at the primary monitoring point.

Will there be any interfaced alarm trigger points?

As a video system grows and becomes more complex due to added cameras and monitors it may be come advantageous to install straining devices, door contacts infrared motion detectors, photo beams, etc to trigger a single camera onto the screen only when an intruder or motion is detected in an area. The strongest advantage of this method of video viewing is that the operator only needs to be concerned with the video system in the event of an actual alarm.

Will there be one, two, or more monitors connected to the same switcher?

As was discussed under point two in this section, one or two monitor points on the same switcher will require the use of bridging and/or looping switchers. If the end user needs four, five, eight, or sixty eight monitors tied into the same switching point with individual control for each monitor as to the cameras viewed, dwell time, alarm input, etc, it would be best to consider microprocessor controlled video switching systems. With the newer microprocessor based switchers, it is easy to achieve all of the above mentioned features and many more for each switcher control points.

Will it be necessary to have individual switching times between cameras?

The average off-the-shelf switcher will provide a single constant switching time for each camera. If the video system under design requires each camera to have its own switching time according to priority, it will be important to note this up front in the ordering of the equipment.

Example: Camera 1 is a priority camera and should be viewed the majority of the time. Cameras 2, 3, 4 are secondary cameras and do not require constant viewing. With individual dwell adjustments, camera 1 can be set 15 seconds per view while cameras 2, 3, and 4 are adjusted for only three seconds of viewing time each.

Will the switcher be required to trip any other devices such as recorders, buzzers, lights, etc, in the event of an alarm?

Pulling up a camera in the event of an alarm has been discussed. However after the camera is pulled up on the screen will there be any other actions deemed necessary at the same time? If the time lapse video recorder is in extreme time lapse mode during an alarm a lot of valuable information could be lost, if however the switcher were to provide it a pulse of electrical information, in the event of an alarm, to the video recorder, the recorder could then be brought up to real time recording during the alarm, enhancing the recording with added information.

Are there plans to expand this system in the future and if yes, will there be room in this switching system to handle the expansion? Common sense should be the rule in this application. If the system that is presently being designed has four cameras, a four position switcher may be all that is needed. If however the system will be updated within a year to eight cameras it would be more cost effective for the customer to purchase the eight position switcher up front.

Will this unit need to be rack mounted or table top? A simple decision to be made based upon location and acted upon during the ordering process of the video equipment.

Quad Splitters

In a system where an extreme number of cameras do not permit the use of only four monitors, such peripherals as the quad splitter or video switchers with alarm input capability may be used.

A quad splitter gives the operator the ability to monitor four cameras on a single careen, in the event that one of the four cameras being viewed needs a closer inspection or larger view, it may be called onto the full screen by itself or the larger single camera picture may be transmitted to the master monitor of the system. Alarm inputs on quad systems allow individual cameras to be pulled up onto the master monitor in the event of an alarm. This would be the best process since the operator will not have to continually view any single monitor for action, thus viewing insensitivity by the operator will be delayed.

Door contact photo beams, passive infrared microwave video motion detectors, floor mats, etc. can be used as the alarm input to trigger a particular camera to be called onto the master monitor. Each type of detection has its own set of standards and rules. All that is needed under most conditions is a dry contact closure to trip the video alarm input to a video switcher and/or a quad splitter.

Quad splitters are best used for video verification as opposed to video identification verification through the use of one or more quad units. It gives the operator the ability to verify that there are pictures at each camera point but not to identify what is happening. The obvious advantage is to be able to monitor several points simultaneously. A second or master work monitor could be used for ID purposes with any other type of switching system.

Terminology

Alarm Call–Up: (auto homing) A feature which enables homing or bridging functions to be imitated by external switch closures from door contacts, motion detectors, photo beams, and/or other types of break detectors. Switchers of this type usually have an external dry contact output to trip other peripheral equipment in the system such as recorders, lights, and/or buzzers in the event of an alarm call–up.

Bridiging: A feature that gives the operator the opportunity to observe two monitors at the same time monitor 1 (A) will display a continuous sequence of pictures from the system while monitor 2 (B) will display a single camera according to the operator's choice. All sequenced pictures will display in an ascending order.

Looping (Input): A feature which provides, in addition to the monitor output (s), a video output for each camera input. This enables the video from each camera to be fed from the switcher to other video equipments. The video line must be terminated at some point beyond the switcher. Switchers without this feature provide the accessory video line termination internally.

Looping Bridging Switchers: Identical to the bridging switcher except that provisions are available for looping the inputs through the switcher to other video equipment such as the homing switcher.

Hold: (home camera lock) A feature that gives the operator the ability to stop the sequence of pictures in order to independently view a single video picture.

Bypass: (skip) A feature that gives the operator the ability to delete and/or skip a particular camera from the sequence switching. Switchers with this feature that have alarm call up will generally call up an alarmed camera input for review even if the alarmed camera in the bypass (skip) mode.

Dwell Time: The dwell time is usually identical for all camera inputs and is controllable by the operator. Independent dwell time adjustment for individual inputs is available in the larger microprocessor controlled units.

Character Display: A feature built into the switcher to input a number and/or letter into the video picture produced by the camera and displayed on the monitor screen for identification purposes. Some switchers with this feature have the ability of operator control of the exact position of the number and/or letter to be displayed in the picture.

External Vertical Switching: This feature allows the operator to hard wire connect a compatible time lapse recorder with the proper output to synchronize the switching of cameras with the actual recording pulse. This feature guarantees a set number of fields per camera recorded despite the speed with which the recorder is run; this is particularly advantageous to systems that are designed with the recorder increasing speed during alarm mode operations.

Vertical Interval Switching: This feature is built in on most new and higher quality units. It enables the unit to do all switching during the vertical blanking of the video signals thus providing a smooth transition, free from roll or flutter. This feature will not correct power phasing problems between cameras causing rolling of pictures during sequencing.

Remote Switchers: Where cameras are located reasonably close to each other but the control and viewing point is distant. Remote versions of the above switchers are available and can offer substantial savings in video cabling. The remote versions include two devices; a remote unit containing the switching functions to be located central to the cameras and a control unit to be located at the control viewing console. The two units are interconnected by multi-conductor cable or twisted pair.

Industrial Recorders Versus Consumer VCRS

When dealing with an industrial time lapse video recorder, there are five different directions that you must view it from, in order to understand and use it properly, both in application and design.

1. Industrial time lapse recorders are designed to operate 24 hours per day, 365 days a year under continuous use. For this reason, their capabilities, cost, design, and environment cannot, under any circumstances, be compared to consumer units.
2. Industrial time lapse recorders, as with any video recorder, are susceptible to overheat and dirty environments and so need

consideration as to their physical positioning within the closed circuit video system.

3. Industrial time lapse recorders are available with multiple options such as dry contact alarm interface, seven day programmable timing circuits, real time to 999 hours continuous recording on two hour tapes, etc. For this reason it is the job of the sales person and the right of the customer to apply the proper machine to the proper job without a lot of overkill.
4. Industrial time lapse recorders should not under any circumstances, use standard or even high-grade consumer tapes. These machines require only industrial video tapes. Use of any other type of tape in this machine can, and will, cause permanent damage to the recording heads.
5. Under no circumstances can the industrial video recorders available today offer a playback resolution of better than 400 horizontal lines. This means that a camera with 750 line resolution and a monitor of 650 lines of resolution will be worthless on playback, as the picture recorded will only play back at maximum 400 lines.

Now that I have laid down the ground work, let's proceed deeper into this intriguing subject. To start, the video tape used for recording must be examined.

All video tapes are made basically in the same way. They consist of a slice of continuous plastic film coated with finely ground metal material such as rust. A video tape is recorded on through a process of low level magnetic pulses applied against the video tape. The coating of rust on the video tape becomes magnetized as a video head is passed by it.

Since the video recording head produces such a low level of magnetic force when recording, it must literally touch the tape as it passes to properly record a field of information.

Pan / Tilts and Their Controllers

Field of View and Purpose of Installation

Although the purpose of the pan and pan/tilt unit seems obvious, you must scratch beneath the surface. By this I mean that the pan or pan/tilt unit is more than a piece of equipment designed to move the camera up and down or side to side. It is a tool that is used to enhance or develop the overall system.

Unfortunately, the pan and pan/tilt units are used far too often to take up the gap in poorly designed systems and/or low budget operations.

A common misconception is that the pan unit can take the place of cameras by having a single camera that can watch multiple points at a time. In a low security profile, the above statement may be true. If the customer is not concerned about blind sports in his/her overall video protection, a pan unit can offer multiple observations from a single camera.

Under normal circumstances the panning camera should not pan a width or a section of view that is wider than its widest point in full wide angle.

The majority of video systems in the field today that have pan/ tilt units are designed and adjusted to sweep an area as wide as 359 degrees or full circle. A downfall in this type of system is that the effective viewing distance of the camera does not match the time it takes to swing the camera around.

If the system that the pan unit is installed in is a low security monitoring point type where the sole purpose of the camera is to visibly spot check various points with no great importance stressed for actual catch viewing, then 359 degree viewing is fine.

The new attraction to the panning community is the 360 degree continuous-spin pan, pan/tilt units. Until lately, the majority of application pan units could spin to the left 359 degrees and then had to spin completely around to the right, and then back. If a standard unit is adjusted to full pan (359 degrees), the spin time from right to left alone allows many things to happen unobserved. With the newer 360 degree continuous spin units, the above situation does not happen since these units can spin around and around without cable restrictions.

High-speed pan units are becoming very popular to help combat limited area viewing also. These units are capable of moving at a rate of 11 degrees per second versus the standard of 3 degrees per second. This increased rate of speed allows the operator to swing the camera around very quickly and will greatly enhance the total viewing area that is feasible with a single camera.

Auto pan is the capability of the panning unit to spin from right to left and back on a continuous sweep automatically. The units are then stopped when something is seen or a when a situation needs to be viewed more closely.

Auto pan is the worst application to be used by any customer. It wears the panning unit out at a percentage rate in proportion to the time in auto pan mode, and it cuts down the effective viewing of the camera. I, or anyone else, can watch the camera swing to the left and know that there will be X amount of time before the unit comes back into my viewing area. A lot can happen in a very short period of time. If the panning span of the camera is short enough, then auto pan can be very effective. However, most applications would work better if a second or third camera were installed.

Random panning is a new form of auto panning with the unit or controller stopping the camera through the panning cycle at different intervals, allowing the operator to view individual points along the scan cycle. It really does not help the auto pan problem. If the area that is being scanned by the pan unit is too wide, all the tricks in the world will not correct it.

A second random panning feature is to pan right X degrees, stop, pan left X degrees, stop, return right X degrees, etc. This feature does give the impression to the outsider that there is human intervention with the camera viewing area, but it still leaves, auto pan as auto pan.

Site Assessment

The following pages are checklists to be used in CCTV systems site assessment.

They are designed to ask all the pertinent questions that need to be answered before the system can be designed, sold, installed, or used.

Although it may seem a great pain to answer each question on each page, the effort will more than pay for itself. What you will find is that the system will more or less design itself and all you will need to do is add the model numbers.

The first of the survey or assessment sheets is the customer form. This form will help you to pinpoint your customer's exact needs at the start of the project. This form can be very valuable down the road when your customer changes his/her mind without remembering the original conversation. It will also help you to keep a perspective on the layout so that you neither short the system nor create overkill.

The next form you will find is for the cameras. Each camera in the system needs a separate form.

The next form is for monitors. This form, in conjunction with all the other information, will help you to assign all the functions necessary to the system to each monitor in a neat and systematic manner.

The fourth for is the accessories form. This form is used for pan/tilt units, housing, and brackets. Each camera requiring any of the above should have a completed form.

The final in this workbook is for all camera locations that may require special lighting. Each camera that will require special lighting should have this form filled out completely.

Upon completion of the site survey, you will have two to four forms per camera location, depending upon requirements of each location. Form these sheets of information, it is a simple matter to piece the entire system together into a system.

If you take the time to learn to work with these forms, you will find that your systems will be sold with a higher ratio of success and professionalism. You will also receive the added benefit of fewer last minute details that cause the customer aggravation, because of extra money he/she has to spend.

Industrial Closed Video System Assessment Check List

Company Name: --

Address: ------------------------------------ Phone: ------------------------------

City: ------------------------------State: --------------Zip: -------------------

Contact: ------------------------Title: ---

1. What is the customers objective: --

   ----

2. What does the customer expect to view: --------------------------------------

   ----

3. What is the customer's budget planning for this project (if available)? $

   ----

4. How many areas are to be viewed by the video system? -------------------

   ----

   List all areas in detail on the back of this page. Include objective of each, i.e. personnel identification, intrusion attempts, movement of object, etc.

		YES	NO	N/A
5.	Is the complete system to be contained within a single building and/or complex?	------	------	-----
5a.	If no, how many buildings will make up the complete system?	------	------	-----
6.	Is this system an add-on to an existing system?	------	------	-----
6a.	If yes, are the blueprints on the original system available?	------	------	-----
7.	Will there be more than one monitoring point?	------	------	-----
7a.	If yes how many monitor points will here be?	------	------	-----

8. Will this system be monitored by personnel? ------ ------ -----
9. Should this system be automated by time? ------ ------ -----
10. Will the customer provide any special power needed for the system? ------ ------ -----
10a. If yes, will the customer handle contracting personnel necessary to complete the wiring? ------ ------ -----
11. Will the customer require additional training on system operation for security personnel? ------ ------ -----

Camera system number or reference code: ----------------------------------

Location: --

Objective viewing area :--

Primary viewing target: ---

Priority of viewing in overall system on scale of 1 to 10, with 10 highest:

Will this camera require a zoom or a fixed focal length lens? --------------

----

Farthest distance to be viewed: -------------------------------- Closest distance to be viewed: ---

Field of view needed at farthest distance: ------------------------------------

----

Width: Height:

Field of view needed at closest distance: --------------------------------------

----

Width: Height:

Are there any buildings, plant life, or other objects obstructing the viewing area: ---

----

What hours will the camera will be monitored

by personnel? by recorder?

From: ---------to: --------- from: -----------to--------------

From: ---------to: ---------- from: -----------to--------------

What type of environment will the camera be mounted in? ---------------

----

Will camera be mounted outside or inside? --------------------------------

----

Type of lighting available day: --------------night: -----------------

Will special lighting be needed at any point of viewing the area? -----------------------------------Where: -------------------------------------

Does this camera need to move?

Up/down: -------------------------- left/right: -------------------------------

Will this camera need a tower or special mount designed and/or built?

What surface will the camera be mounted on, i.e. wall, ceiling, corner?

Is there power available at the camera site? --------------------what type?

What is the distance from the camera to the monitoring site? -------------

----

Is there a clear route for coaxial cable? ----------------Pole, ceiling, underground: ---

----

If cable is not applicable, is there a clear line of sight? --------------------

----

Make a rough sketch of the area of mounting and viewing on the back side of this page.

Site Survey Cabling, Houseing, Brackets, PAN/TILTS

Camera #:-------------------------

I. CABLING

1. What is the distance between this camera and the first termination point?

---

2. Will there be multiple termination points in this cable run? ---

---

3. If yes, what is the total distance between the camera and the final termination point? ---
4. What size of cable will be needed for the camera? ---
5. If cabling is not used, what will be the method of transmission? ---

---

II. HOUSING

1. What is the overall length of this camera complete with lens? ---

---

2. Will this camera be installed outside or inside? ---
3. Will this camera require special protection due to dust, temperature, humidity? ---
4. Are there any building obstructions preventing this housing from being opened from: top? --- bottom? --- left side? --- right side? --- front? --- back? ---
5. Will this housing need to be designed and built specially? ---

---

If Yes, Include Drawing of Area, Shape, View, and Location with this form.

III. BRACKET

1. What will be the total weight plus 10% of the camera, lens, housing and pan/tilt? ---
2. This bracket will be mounted on: wall? --- ceiling? --- floor? --- corner? ---
3. What type of building material will this bracket be mounted on? ---

---

4. Does this bracket require special rigging to allow swinging for service?

---

5. Does this bracket require design to fit in with building design? ---

----

IV. PAN/TILT

1. What is the total rotation required for this pan/tilt? horizontal ----------
   vertical ---
2. Will this unit require special application of pre-positioning? -------------
   ----
3. What will be the total weight plus 10% of the camera, lens, and housing?
   ----
4. What type of wiring will this unit require for controlling? ----------------
   ----
5. What is the total distance from the controller to the pan/tilt? ------------
   ----

Assessment Check List Lighting Locations

Location: ---

What is the distance of the scene to be viewed from the camera? --------------

----

What is the size of the area requiring additional lighting? --------------------

----

Inside? Height?

Is the application for additional lighting: --

Inside? Outside?

What type of camera is (to be) installed in the area requiring more light?

Is it necessary that the lighting be unnoticeable to the human eye? -----------

----

Is there power available where additional lighting is necessary? ----------------

----

What type? ---

At what height would the lighting need to be installed? ------------------------

----

Will the additional light needed, be a nuisance to the neighbourhood? -------

----

Will the additional light needed be within the light pollution ordinances?

Will a fixture brightness upgrade within the area be sufficient? ---------------

----

What will be the result of light failure in this area? ---------------------------

----

Is the additional light to deter, or to apprehend? -------------------------------

----

Will the glare created by additional lighting cause a problem in the area? ----

----

How much light needs to be added in this area? -------------------------------

----

Assessment Check List Monitor Location

Location: ---

Total number of monitors at this location ---------------------------------------

----

Total monitors by size: 9"-----------------------12"------------------------

15"---------------------19"---------------------21"-----------------------

Total switching monitors: ---------------------------------fixed scene: -------

----------------------- recorded: --

Will these monitors be part of the master system or a remote? ---------------

----

Will these monitors be viewed constantly? ----------------------------------,

by security personnel? --

What type of environment will these monitors be mounted in, i.e. clean, dusty, etc? ---

----

Distance from which the monitors will be viewed: 9"-------------12"------------

15"-----------------------------19"-------------------------- other------------------

Cameras to be assigned to each monitor:

MONITOR 1 ------------------------ MONITOR 2 -------------------------------

MONITOR 3 ------------------------ MONITOR 4 -------------------------------

MONITOR 5 ------------------------ MONITOR 6 -------------------------------

Which monitor (s) if any; will be used in a quad split frame? ------------------

Which monitor (s) if any, will be colour? ---

Which monitor (s) will be dedicated to controlling devices? -------------------

***

Annexure–I
Mumbai Attacks–2008

Summary

Date: 26 November 2008–29 November 2008 (IST, UTC + 05:30)

Attack type: Bombings, shootings, hostage crisis, siege

Deaths: Approximately 202 (including 10 attackers)

Injured: More than 308

Perpetrator: Lashkar-e-Taiba led by Hafiz Muhammad Saeed

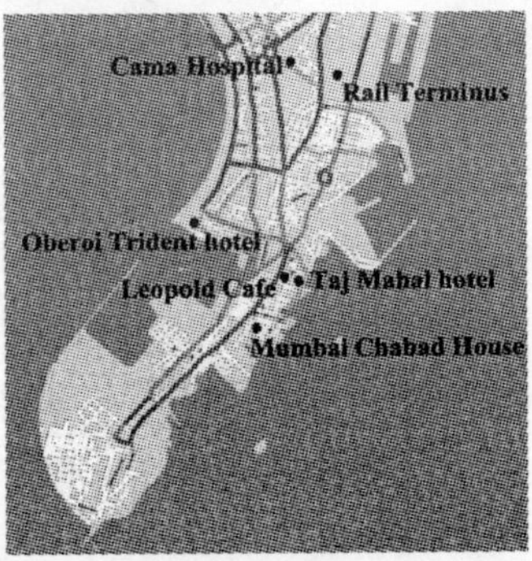

Map of the 2008 Mumbai attacks

The 2008 Mumbai attacks were 11 coordinated shooting and bombing attacks across Mumbai, India's largest city, by terrorists who were trained in, and came from, Pakistan.

The attackers allegedly received reconnaissance assistance before the attacks. Ajmal Kasab, the only attacker who was captured alive later confessed upon interrogation that the attacks were conducted with the support of Pakistan's ISI. The attacks, which drew widespread global condemnation, began on Wednesday, November 26 and lasted until Saturday, 29 November 2008, killing 164 people and wounding at least 308.

Eight of the attacks occurred in South Mumbai: at Chhatrapati Shivaji Terminus, the Oberoi Trident, the Taj Mahal Palace & Tower, Leopold Cafe, Cama Hospital (a women and children's hospital), the Nariman House Jewish community centre, the Metro Cinema, and a lane behind the Times of India building and St. Xavier's College. There was also an explosion at Mazagaon, in Mumbai's port area, and in a taxi at Vile Parle. By the early morning of November 28, all sites except for the Taj hotel had been secured by Mumbai Police and security forces. On 29 November, India's National Security Guards (NSG) conducted Operation Black Tornado to flush out the remaining attackers; it resulted in the deaths of the last remaining attackers at the Taj hotel and ending all fighting in the attacks.

Ajmal Kasab disclosed that the attackers were members of Lashkar-e-Taiba, the Pakistan-based militant organisation, considered a terrorist organisation by India, Pakistan, the United States, the United Kingdom, and the United Nations, among others. The Indian government said that the attackers came from Pakistan, and their controllers were in Pakistan. On 7 January 2009, Pakistan's Information Minister, Sherry Rehman officially accepted Ajmal Kasab's nationality as Pakistani. On 12 February 2009, Pakistan's Interior Minister, Rehman Malik asserted that parts of the attack had been planned in Pakistan. A trial court on 6 May 2010 sentenced Ajmal Kasab to death on five counts.

Attacks

The first events were detailed around 20:00 Indian Standard Time

(IST) on 26 November, when 10 men in inflatable speedboats came ashore at two locations in Colaba. They reportedly told local Marathi-speaking fishermen who asked them who they were, to "mind their own business" before they split up and headed two different ways. The fishermen's subsequent report to police received little response.

Chhatrapati Shivaji Terminus

Bullet marks on the wall of the suburban terminus at CST

The Chhatrapati Shivaji Terminus (CST) was attacked by two gunmen, one of whom, Ajmal Kasab, was later caught alive by the police and identified by eyewitnesses. The attacks began around 21:30 when the two men entered the passenger hall and opened fire, using AK-47 rifles. The attackers killed 58 people and injured 104 others, their assault ending at about 22:45. Security forces and emergency services arrived shortly afterwards. The two gunmen fled the scene and fired at pedestrians and police officers in the streets, killing eight police officers. The attackers passed a police station. Many of the outgunned police officers were afraid to confront the attackers, and instead switched off the lights and secured the gates. The attackers then headed towards Cama Hospital with an intention to kill patients, but the hospital staff locked all of the patient wards. A team of the Mumbai Anti-Terrorist Squad led by police chief Hemant Karkare searched the Chhatrapati Shivaji Terminus and then left in pursuit of Kasab and Khan. Kasab and Khan opened fire on the vehicle in a lane next to the hospital and the police returned fire. Karkare, Vijay Salaskar, Ashok Kamte and one of their officers were killed, though the only survivor, constable Arun Jadhav, was wounded. Kasab and Khan seized the police vehicle but later abandoned it and seized a passenger car instead. They then ran into a police roadblock, which had been set up after Jadhav radioed for help. A gun battle then ensued in which Khan was killed and Kasab was wounded. After a physical struggle, Kasab was arrested. A police officer, Tukaram Omble was also killed.

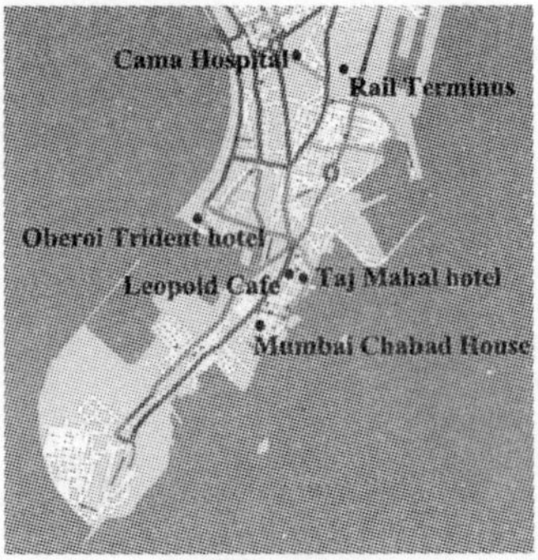

Map of the 2008 Mumbai attacks

Leopold Cafe

The Leopold Cafe, a popular restaurant and bar on Colaba Causeway in South Mumbai, was one of the first sites to be attacked. Two attackers opened fire on the cafe on the evening of 26 November, killing at least 10 people (including some foreigners), and injuring many more. The attackers fired into the street as they fled the scene.

Bullet marks left at Leopold Cafe

Bomb blasts in taxis

There were two explosions in taxis caused by timer bombs. The first one occurred at 22:40 at Vile Parle, killing the driver and a passenger. The second explosion took place at Wadi Bunder between 22:20 and 22:25. Three people including the driver of the taxi were killed, and about 15 other people were injured.

Taj Mahal Hotel and Oberoi Trident

The damaged Oberoi Trident hotel

The Wasabi restaurant on the first floor of the Taj Hotel was completely gutted

Two hotels, the Taj Mahal Palace & Tower and the Oberoi Trident, were amongst the four locations targeted. Six explosions were reported at the Taj hotel - one in the lobby, two in the elevators, three in the restaurant, and one explosion was reported at the Oberoi Trident. At the Taj Mahal, firefighters rescued 200 hostages from windows using ladders during the first night. CNN initially reported on the morning of 27 November 2008 that the hostage situation at the Taj had been resolved and quoted the police chief of Maharashtra stating that all hostages were freed; however, it was learned later that day that there were still two attackers holding hostages, including foreigners, in the Taj Mahal hotel.

During the attacks, both hotels were surrounded by Rapid Action Force personnel and Marine Commandos (MARCOS) and National Security Guards (NSG) commandos. When reports emerged that attackers were receiving television broadcasts, feeds to the hotels were blocked. Security forces stormed both hotels, and all nine attackers were killed by the morning of 29 November. Major Sandeep Unnikrishnan of the NSG was killed during the rescue of Commando Sunil Yadav, who was hit in the leg by a bullet during the rescue operations at Taj. 32 hostages were killed at the Oberoi Trident.

A number of European Parliament Committee on International Trade delegates were staying in the Taj Mahal hotel when it was attacked, but none of them were injured. British Conservative Member of the European Parliament (MEP), Sajjad Karim (who was in the lobby when attackers initially opened fire there) and German Social Democrat MEP, Erika Mann were hiding in different parts of the building. Also reported present was Spanish MEP Ignasi Guardans, who was barricaded in a hotel room. Another British Conservative MEP, Syed Kamall, reported that he, along with several other MEPs, left the hotel and went to a nearby restaurant shortly before the attack. Kamall also reported that Polish MEP Jan Masiel was thought to have been sleeping in his hotel room when the attacks started, but eventually left the hotel safely. Kamall and Guardans reported that a Hungarian MEP's assistant was shot. Also caught up in the shooting were the President of Madrid, Esperanza Aguirre, while checking in at the Oberoi Trident, and Indian MP N. N. Krishnadas of Kerala and Gulam Noon while having dinner at a restaurant in the Taj hotel.

Nariman House

Nariman House, a Chabad Lubavitch Jewish centre in Colaba known as the Mumbai Chabad House, was taken over by two attackers and several residents were held hostage. Police evacuated adjacent buildings and exchanged fire with the attackers, wounding one. Local residents were told to stay inside. The attackers threw a grenade into

Front view of the Nariman House a week after the attacks

a nearby lane, causing no casualties. NSG commandos arrived from Delhi, and a naval helicopter took an aerial survey. During the first day, 9 hostages were rescued from the first floor. The following day, the house was stormed by NSG commandos fast-roping from helicopters onto the roof, covered by snipers positioned in nearby buildings. After a long battle, one NSG commando Havaldar Gajender Singh Bisht, and both perpetrators were killed. Rabbi Gavriel Holtzberg and his wife Rivka Holtzberg, who was six months pregnant, were murdered with four other hostages inside the house by the attackers.

According to radio transmissions picked up by Indian intelligence, the attackers "would be told by their handlers in Pakistan that the lives of Jews were worth 50 times those of non-Jews." Injuries reported on some of the bodies indicate they may have been tortured.

National Security Guards

The National Security Guard (NSG) is a special response unit in India that has primarily been utilized for counter-terrorism activities and was created by the Cabinet Secretariat under the National Security Guard Act of the Indian Parliament in 1986. It works completely within the Central Armed Police Forces structure. The NSG is an elite force providing a second line of defence to the nation. They have played a pivotal role in safeguarding the unity of India and have commendably foiled attempts of anti-national elements to tear apart the social fabric of the country. The NSG has maintained an edge over terrorist outfits in possession of latest technology and are considered among the best special operations units in all of Asia.

End of the attacks

By the morning of 27 November, the NSG had secured the Jewish outreach centre at Nariman House as well as the Oberoi Trident hotel. They also incorrectly believed that the Taj Mahal Palace & Towers had been cleared of attackers, and soldiers were leading hostages and holed up guests to safety, and removing bodies of those killed in the attacks.

However, later news reports indicated that there were still two or three attackers in the Taj, with explosions heard and gunfire exchanged. Fires were also reported at the ground floor of the Taj with plumes of smoke arising from the first floor. The final operation at the Taj Mahal Palace hotel was completed by the NSG commandos at 08:00 on 29 November, killing three attackers and resulting in the conclusion of the attacks. The NSG rescued 250 people from the Oberoi, 300 from the Taj and 60 people (members of 12 different families) from Nariman House. In addition, police seized a boat filled with arms and explosives anchored at Mazgaon dock off Mumbai harbour.

Attribution

Ajmal Kasab, the sole surviving terrorist, at Chhatrapati Shivaji Terminus

The Mumbai attacks were planned and directed by Lashkar-e-Taiba militants inside Pakistan, and carried out by ten young armed men trained and sent to Mumbai, and directed from inside Pakistan via mobile phones and VoIP.

In July 2009, Pakistani authorities confirmed that LeT plotted and financed the attacks from LeT camps in Karachi and Thatta. In November 2009, Pakistani authorities charged seven men they had arrested earlier, of planning and executing the assault.

Mumbai police originally identified 37 suspects—including two army officers—for their alleged involvement in the plot. All but two of the suspects, many of whom are identified only through aliases, are Pakistani. Two more suspects arrested in the United States in October 2009 for other attacks were also found to have been involved in planning the Mumbai attacks. One of these men, Pakistani-American David Headley, was found to have made several trips to India before the attacks and gathered video and GPS information on behalf of the plotters.

In April 2011, the United States issued arrest warrants for four Pakistani men as suspects in the attack. The men, Sajid Mir, Abu Qahafa, Mazhar Iqbal, and alias "Major Iqbal", are believed to be members of Lashkar-e-Taiba, who helped plan and train the attackers.

Negotiations with Pakistan

Pakistan initially denied that Pakistanis were responsible for the attacks, blaming plotters in Bangladesh and Indian criminals, a claim refuted by India, and saying they needed information from India on other bombings first.

Pakistani authorities finally agreed that Ajmal Kasab was a Pakistani on 7 January 2009, and registered a case against three other Pakistani nationals.

The Indian government supplied evidence to Pakistan and other governments, in the form of interrogations, weapons, and call records of conversations during the attacks. In addition, Indian government officials said that the attacks were so sophisticated that they must have had official backing from Pakistani 'agencies', an accusation denied by Pakistan.

Under US and UN pressure, Pakistan arrested a few members of Jamaat ud-Dawa and briefly put its founder under house arrest, but he was found to be free a few days later. A year after the attacks,

Mumbai police continued to complain that Pakistani authorities are not cooperating by providing information for their investigation. Meanwhile, journalists in Pakistan said security agencies were preventing them from interviewing people from Kasab's village. Home Minister P. Chidambaram said the Pakistani authorities had not shared any information about American suspects Headley and Rana, but that the FBI had been more forthcoming.

An Indian report, summarising intelligence gained from India's interrogation of David Headley, was released in October 2010. It alleged that Pakistan's intelligence agency (ISI) had provided support for the attacks by providing funding for reconnaissance missions in Mumbai. The report included Headley's claim that Lashkar-e-Taiba's chief military commander, Zaki-ur-Rahman Lakhvi, had close ties to the ISI. He alleged that 'every big action of LeT is done in close coordination with [the] ISI."

Investigation

Police looking for attackers outside Colaba

According to investigations, the attackers travelled by sea from Karachi, Pakistan, across the Arabian Sea, hijacked the Indian fishing trawler 'Kuber', killed the crew of four, then forced the captain to sail to Mumbai. After murdering the captain, the attackers entered Mumbai on a rubber dinghy. The captain of 'Kuber', Amar Singh

Solanki, had earlier been imprisoned for six months in a Pakistani jail for illegally fishing in Pakistani waters. The attackers stayed, and were trained by the Lashkar-e-Taiba, in a safehouse at Azizabad near Karachi before boarding a small boat for Mumbai.

David Headley was a member of Lashkar-e-Taiba, and between 2002 and 2009 Headley travelled extensively as part of his work for LeT. Headley received training in small arms and counter-surveillance from LeT, built a network of connections for the group, and was chief scout in scoping out targets for Mumbai attack having allegedly been given $25,000 in cash in 2006 by an ISI officer known as Major Iqbal, The officer also helped him arrange a communication system for the attack, and oversaw a model of the Taj Mahal Hotel so that gunmen could know their way inside the target, according to Headley's testimony to Indian authorities. Headley also helped ISI recruit Indian agents to monitor Indian troop levels and movements, according to a US official. At the same time, Headley was also an informant for the U.S. Drug Enforcement Administration, and Headley's wives warned American officials of Headley's involvement with LeT and his plotting attacks, warning specifically that the Taj Mahal Hotel may be their target.

US officials believed that the Inter Services Intelligence (ISI) officers provided support to Lashkar-e-Taiba militants who carried out the attacks.

The arrest of Zabiuddin Ansari alias Abu Hamza in June 2012 provided further clarity on how the plot was hatched. According to Abu Hamza, the attacks were previously scheduled for 2006, using an Indian youth for the job. However, a huge cache of AK-47's and RDX, which were to be used for the attacks, was recovered from Aurangabad in 2006 thus leading to the dismantling of the original plot. Subsequently, Abu Hamza fled to Pakistan and along with Lashkar commanders, scouted for Pakistani youth to be used the attacks. In September 2007, ten people were selected for the mission. In September 2008, these people tried sailing to Mumbai from Karachi, but couldn't complete their mission due to choppy waters. These men made a second attempt in November 2008, and successfully managed to execute the final attacks. David Headley's disclosures that three Pakistani army officers were associated with the planning and execution of the attack were substantiated by Ansari's revelations during his interrogation. After Ansari's arrest, Pakistan's Foreign Office claimed they had received information that up to 40 Indian nationals were involved in the attacks.

Method

The attackers had planned the attack several months ahead of time and knew some areas well enough for the attackers to vanish, and reappear after security forces had left. Several sources have quoted Kasab telling the police that the group received help from Mumbai residents. The attackers used at least three SIM cards purchased on the Indian side of the border with Bangladesh. There were also reports of a SIM card purchased in the US state of New Jersey. Police had also mentioned that Faheem Ansari, an Indian Lashkar operative who had been arrested in February 2008, had scouted the Mumbai targets for the November attacks. Later, the police arrested two Indian suspects, Mikhtar Ahmad, who is from Srinagar in Kashmir, and Tausif Rehman, a resident of Kolkata. They supplied the SIM cards, one in Calcutta, and the other in New Delhi.

Type 86 Grenades made by China's state-owned Norinco were used in the attacks.

Blood tests on the attackers indicate that they had taken cocaine and LSD during the attacks, to sustain their energy and stay awake for 50 hours. Police say that they found syringes on the scenes of the attacks. There were also indications that they had been taking steroids. The gunman who survived said that the attackers had used

Google Earth to familiarise themselves with the locations of buildings used in the attacks.

There were ten gunmen, nine of whom were subsequently shot dead and one captured by security forces. Witnesses reported that they looked to be in their early twenties, wore black t-shirts and jeans, and that they smiled and looked happy as they shot their victims.

It was initially reported that some of the attackers were British citizens, but the Indian government later stated that there was no evidence to confirm this. Similarly, early reports of twelve gunmen were also later shown to be incorrect.

On 9 December, the ten attackers were identified by Mumbai police, along with their home towns in Pakistan: Ajmal Amir from Faridkot, Abu Ismail Dera Ismail Khan from Dera Ismail Khan, Hafiz Arshad and Babr Imran from Multan, Javed from Okara, Shoaib from Narowal, Nazih and Nasr from Faisalabad, Abdul Rahman from Arifwalla, and Fahad Ullah from Dipalpur Taluka. Dera Ismail Khan is in the North-West Frontier Province; the rest of the towns are in Pakistani Punjab.

On 6 April 2010, the Home Minister of Maharashtra State, which includes Mumbai, informed the assembly that the bodies of the nine killed Pakistani gunmen from the 2008 attack on Mumbai were buried in a secret location in January 2010. The bodies had been in the mortuary of a Mumbai hospital after Muslim clerics in the city refused to let them be buried on their grounds.

Arrests

Ajmal Kasab was the only attacker arrested alive by police and is currently under arrest. Much of the information about the attackers' preparation, travel, and movements comes from his confessions to the Mumbai police.

On 12 February 2009 Pakistan's Interior Minister Rehman Malik said that Pakistani national Javed Iqbal, who acquired VoIP phones in Spain for the Mumbai attackers, and Hamad Ameen Sadiq, who had facilitated money transfer for the attack, had been arrested. Two other men known as Khan and Riaz, but whose full names were not given, were also arrested. Two Pakistanis were arrested in Brescia, Italy (north-west of Milan), on 21 November 2009, after being accused of providing logistical support to the attacks and transferring over US$200 to internet accounts using a false ID. They had Red Corner Notices issued against them by Interpol for their suspected involvement and it was issued after the last year's strikes.

In October 2009, two Chicago men were arrested and charged by the FBI for involvement in terrorism abroad, David Coleman Headley and Tahawwur Hussain Rana. Headley, a Pakistani-American, was charged in November 2009 with scouting locations for the 2008 Mumbai attacks. Headley is reported to have posed as an American Jew and is believed to have links with militant Islamist groups based in Bangladesh. On 18 March 2010, Headley pled guilty to a dozen charges against him thereby avoiding going to trial.

In December 2009, the FBI charged Abdur Rehman Hashim Syed, a retired major in the Pakistani army, for planning the terror attacks in association with Headley.

On 15 January 2010, in a successful snatch operation RAW agents nabbed Sheikh Abdul Khwaja, one of the handlers of the 26/11 attacks, chief of HUJI India operations and a most-wanted terror suspect in India, from Colombo, Sri Lanka, and brought him over to Hyderabad, India for formal arrest.

On 25 June 2012, the Delhi Police arrested Zabiuddin Ansari alias Abu Hamza, one of the key suspects in the attack at the Indira Gandhi International Airport in New Delhi. His arrest was touted as the most significant development in the case since Kasab's arrest. Security agencies had been chasing him for 3 years in Delhi. Ansari is a Lashker-e-Taiba ultra and the Hindi tutor of 10 terrorists who were responsible for the Mumbai attacks in 2008.

He was apprehended, after he was arrested and deported to India by Saudi Intelligence officials as per official request by Indian authorities.

After Ansari's arrest, investigations revealed that in 2009 he allegedly stayed for a day in a room in Old Legislators's Hostel, belonging to Fauzia Khan, a former MLA and minister in Maharashtra Government. The minister, however, denied having any links with him. Home Minister P Chidambaram, asserted that Ansari was provided safe place in Pakistan and was present in the control room which could not be established without active State support. Ansari's interrogation further revealed that Sajid Mir and a Pakistani Army major visited India under fake names as cricket spectators to survey targets in Delhi and Mumbai for about a fortnight.

Casualties and Compensation

At least 266 victims (civilians and security personnel) and nine attackers were killed in the attacks. Among the dead were 28 foreign nationals from 10 countries. One attacker was captured. The bodies of many of the dead hostages showed signs of torture or disfigurement. A number of those killed were notable figures in business, media, and security services.

The government of Maharashtra announced about 500,000 (US$9,050) as compensation to the kin of each of those killed in the terror attacks and about 50,000 (US$905) to the seriously injured. In August 2009, Indian Hotels Company and the Oberoi Group received about $28 million USD as part-payment of the insurance claims, on account of the attacks on Taj Mahal and Trident, from General Insurance Corporation of India.

Aftermath

The attacks are sometimes referred to in India as "26/11", after the date in 2008 that they began and the nomenclature behind the 9/11 attacks (akin to that of the 3/11 attack in Madrid). The Pradhan Inquiry Commission, appointed by the Maharashtra government, produced a report that was tabled before the legislative assembly over one year after the events. The report said the "war-like" attack was beyond the capacity of any police force, but it also found fault with the Mumbai Police Commissioner Hasan Gafoor's lack of leadership during the crisis.

The Maharashtra government planned to buy 36 speed boats to patrol the coastal areas and several helicopters for the same purpose. It also planned to create an anti-terror force called "Force One" and upgrade all the weapons that Mumbai police currently have. Prime Minister Manmohan Singh on an all-party conference declared that legal framework would be strengthened in the battle against terrorism and a federal anti-terrorist intelligence and investigation agency, like the FBI, will be set up soon to coordinate action against terrorism. The government strengthened anti-terror laws with UAPA 2008, and the federal National Investigation Agency was formed.

The attacks further strained India's slowly recovering relationship with Pakistan. External Affairs Minister Pranab Mukherjee declared that India may indulge in military strikes against terror camps in Pakistan to protect its territorial integrity. There were also after-effects on the United States' relationship with both countries, the US-led NATO war in Afghanistan, and on the Global War on Terror. FBI chief Robert Mueller praised the "unprecedented cooperation" between American and Indian intelligence agencies over Mumbai terror attack probe. Interpol secretary general Ronald Noble indicated Indian intelligence agencies did not share any information with them.

Movement of Troops

Pakistan moved troops towards the border with India, voicing concerns about the Indian government's possible plans to launch attacks on Pakistani soil if it did not cooperate. After days of talks, the Pakistan government, however, decided to start moving troops away from the border.

Reactions

Candlelight vigils at the Gateway of India in Mumbai

Indians criticized their political leaders after the attacks, saying that their ineptness was partly responsible. The Times of India commented on its front page that 'Our politicians fiddle as innocents die.' Political reactions in Mumbai and India included a range of resignations and political changes, including the resignations of Minister for Home Affairs Shivraj Patil, Chief Minister Vilasrao Deshmukh and Deputy Chief Minister R R Patil for controversial reactions to the attack including taking the former's son and Bollywood director Ram Gopal Verma to tour the damaged Taj Mahal and the latter's remarks that the attacks were not a big deal in such a large city. Prominent Muslim personalities such as Bollywood actor Aamir Khan appealed to their community members in the country to observe Eid al-Adha as a day of mourning on December 9. The business establishment also reacted, with changes to transport, and requests for an increase in self-defense capabilities. The attacks also triggered a chain of citizens' movements across India such as the India Today Group's "War Against Terror" campaign. There were vigils held across all of India with candles and placards commemorating the victims of the attacks. The NSG commandos based in Delhi also met criticism for taking 10 hours to reach the 3 sites under attack.

Citizens gather outside the Taj Mahal Palace & Tower hotel demanding the government takes action.

International reaction for the attacks was widespread, with many countries and international organisations condemning the attacks and expressing their condolences to the civilian victims. Many important personalities around the world also condemned the attacks.

Media coverage highlighted the use of social media and Internet social networking tools, including Twitter and Flickr, in spreading information about the attacks. In addition, many Indian bloggers offered live textual coverage of the attacks. A map of the attacks was set up by a web journalist using Google Maps.

The New York Times, in July 2009, described the event as "what may be the most well-documented terrorist attack anywhere."

In November 2010, families of American victims of the attacks filed a lawsuit in Brooklyn, New York, naming Lt. Gen. Ahmed Shuja Pasha, chief of the ISI, as being complicit in the Mumbai attacks. On 22 September 2011, the attack on the American Embassy in Afghanistan, was attributed to Pakistan via cell phone records identical to the attacks in Mumbai, also linked to Pakistan. The investigation is on-going.

Trials

Kasab's trial

Kasab's trial was delayed due to legal issues, as many Indian lawyers were unwilling to represent him. A Mumbai Bar Association passed a resolution proclaiming that none of its members would represent Kasab. However, the Chief Justice of India stated that Kasab needed a lawyer for a fair trial. A lawyer for Kasab was eventually found, but was replaced due to a conflict of interest. On 25 February 2009, Indian investigators filed an 11,000-page chargesheet, formally charging Kasab with murder, conspiracy, and waging war against India among other charges.

Kasab's trial began on 6 May 2009. He initially pleaded not guilty, but later admitted his guilt on 20 July 2009. He initially apologized for the attacks and claimed that he deserved the death penalty for his crimes, but later retracted these claims, saying that he had been tortured by police to force his confession, and that he had been arrested while roaming on the beach. The court had accepted his plea, but due to the lack of completeness within his admittance, the judge had deemed that many of the 86 charges were not addressed and therefore the trial continued.

Kasab was convicted of all 86 charges on 3 May 2010. He was found guilty of murder for directly killing seven people, conspiracy to commit murder for the deaths of the 166 people killed in the three-day terror siege, waging war against India, causing terror, and of conspiracy to murder two high-ranking police officers. On 6 May 2010, he was sentenced to death by hanging. However, he appealed his sentence at high court. On 21 February 2011, the Bombay High Court upheld the death sentence of Kasab, dismissing his appeal.

Trials in Pakistan

Indian and Pakistani police have exchanged DNA evidence, photographs and items found with the attackers to piece together a detailed portrait of the Mumbai plot. Police in Pakistan have arrested seven people, including Hammad Amin Sadiq, a homoeopathic pharmacist, who arranged bank accounts and secured supplies. Sadiq and six others begin their formal trial on 3 October 2009 in Pakistan, though Indian authorities say the prosecution stops well short of top Lashkar leaders. In November 2009, Indian Prime Minister Manmohan Singh said that Pakistan has not done enough to bring the perpetrators of the attacks to justice.

On the eve of the first anniversary of 26/11, a Pakistani anti-terror court formally charged seven accused, including LeT operations commander Zaki ur Rehman Lakhvi. However the actual trial started on 5th may 2012. The Pakistani court conducting trial of Mumbai attacks accused, reserved its judgement on the application filed by Lakhvi, challenging the report of the judicial panel, to 17 July 2012. On 17 July 2012, the court refused to take the findings of the Pakistani judicial commission as part of the evidence. It however, ruled that if a new agreement that allows the panel's examination of witnesses, is reached, the prosecution may move an application for sending the panel to Mumbai. The Indian Government upset over the court ruling, however, contended that evidence collected by the Pakistani judicial panel has evidential value to punish all those involved in the attack. On 28 July 2012, a Pakistani court conducting the trial of seven terror suspects charged with involvement in the Mumbai attacks did not record the statements of two prosecution witnesses following legal objections raised by defence lawyers to their testimony. The judge accepted their argument that the statements of the two FIA officials should not be recorded as the anti-terrorism court had already rejected the report prepared by a Pakistani judicial commission that visited Mumbai to probe the attacks.

Trials in USA

The LeT operative David Headley in his testimony before a Chicago federal court during co-accused Tahawwur Rana's trial revealed that Mumbai Chabad House was added to the list of targets for surveillance given by his Inter Services Intelligence handler Major Iqbal, though the Oberoi hotel, one of the sites attacked, was not originally on the list. On 10 June 2011, Tahawwur Rana was acquitted of plotting the 2008 Mumbai attacks, but was held guilty on two other charges.

References

1. Magnier, Mark; Sharma, Subhash (27 November 2008). "India terrorist attacks leave at least 101 dead in Mumbai". Los Angeles Times: p. A1. Retrieved 28 November 2008.
2. a b c d "HM announces measures to enhance security"(Press release). Press Information Bureau (Government of India). 11 December 2008. Retrieved 14 December 2008.
3. a b c Somini Sengupta (6 January 2009). "Dossier From India Gives New Details of Mumbai Attacks". The New York Times.Archived from the original on 21 February 2009. Retrieved 14 February 2009.
4. Rahman, Maseeh (27 November 2008). "Mumbai terror attacks: Who could be behind them?". The Guardian (UK).Archived from the original on 5 December 2008. Retrieved 29 November 2008.
5. Friedman, Thomas (17 February 2009). "No Way, No How, Not Here". The New York Times. Archived from the original on 20 April 2010. Retrieved 17 May 2010.
6. Indian Muslims hailed for not burying 26/11 attackers, Sify News, 19 February 2009, retrieved 15 July 2011
7. Schifrin, Nick (25 November 2009). "Mumbai Terror Attacks: 7 Pakistanis Charged – Action Comes a Year After India's Worst Terrorist Attacks; 166 Die.". ABC News. Retrieved 17 May 2010.
8. Accused in India massacre claims ties to Pakistani secret service The Globe and Mail, 11 Apr. 2011 11:15 pm EDT
9. Rana, Headley implicate Pak, ISI in Mumbai attack during ISI chief's

visit to US The Times of India, 12 Apr 2011, 12.13 pm IST

10. Black, Ian (28 November 2008). "Attacks draw worldwide condemnation". The Guardian (UK). Archived from the original on 1 December 2008. Retrieved 5 December 2008.
11. a b c d "Wave of Terror Attacks Strikes India's Mumbai, Killing at Least 182". Fox News. 27 November 2008. Archivedfrom the original on 4 December 2008. Retrieved 3 December 2008.
12. Kahn, Jeremy (2 December 2008). "Jews of Mumbai, a Tiny and Eclectic Group, Suddenly Reconsider Their Serene Existence". New York Times. Archived from the original on 6 December 2008. Retrieved 3 December 2008.
13. Magnier, Mark (3 December 2008). "Mumbai police officers describe nightmare of attack". Los Angeles Times. Archived from the original on 6 December 2008. Retrieved 3 December 2008.
14. a b "Tracing the terror route". The Indian Express (India). 10 December 2008. Archived from the original on 28 May 2009. Retrieved 9 December 2008.
15. "Police declare Mumbai siege over". BBC. 29 November 2008. Archived from the original on 29 November 2008. Retrieved 29 November 2008.
16. "Terrorist's name lost in transliteration". The Hindu(Chennai, India). 6 December 2008. Archived from the original on 8 December 2008. Retrieved 7 December 2008.
17. "Lashkar-e-Taiba (Army of the Pure) (aka Lashkar e-Tayyiba, Lashkar e-Toiba; Lashkar-i-Taiba)–Council on Foreign Relations". Cfr.org. Archived from the original on 8 January 2011. Retrieved 31 December 2010.
18. a b Schmitt, Eric; Somini Sengupta, Jane Perlez (3 December 2008). "US and India See Link to Militants in Pakistan". New York Times. Retrieved 3 December 2008.
19. Somini Sengupta and Eric Schmitt (3 December 2008). "Ex-US Official Cites Pakistani Training for India Attackers". The New York Times. Archived from the original on 9 February 2009. Retrieved 14 February 2009.

20. a b "Pakistan Continues to Resist India Pressure on Mumbai". TIME. 8 January 2009. Archived from the original on 14 January 2009. Retrieved 8 January 2009.
21. "Surviving gunman's identity established as Pakistani".Dawn. 7 January 2009. Archived from the original on 28 May 2009. Retrieved 7 January 2009.
22. Masood, Salman (13 February 2009). "Pakistan Says Mumbai Attack Partly Planned on Its Soil". The New York Times. Retrieved 14 February 2009.
23. a b "26/11: Kasab guilty; Ansari, Sabauddin Shaikh acquitted". The Times of India (India). 3 May 2010. Retrieved 4 May 2010.
24. a b "With HC order, Kasab one step closer to gallows". The Times of India (India). 22 February 2011. Retrieved 22 February 2011.
25. a b Patnaik, Pratap (29 August 2012). "Death Sentence for Mumbai Gunman Upheld by India's Supreme Court". Bloomberg Businessweek. Retrieved 29 August 2012.
26. "1993: Bombay hit by devastating bombs". BBC. 12 March 1993. Archived from the original on 11 December 2008. Retrieved 12 November 2008.
27. Monica Chadha (12 September 2006). "Victims await Mumbai 1993 blasts justice". BBC. Archived from the original on 10 December 2008. Retrieved 12 November 2008.
28. "Blast outside Ghatkopar station in Mumbai, 2 killed".rediff.com India Limited. 6 December 2002. Retrieved 19 August 2008.
29. "1992: Mob rips apart mosque in Ayodhya". BBC. 6 December 1992. Archived from the original on 7 December 2008. Retrieved 11 November 2008.
30. "1 killed, 25 hurt in Vile Parle blast". The Times of India(India). 28 January 2003. Retrieved 19 August 2008.
31. "Fear after Bombay train blast". BBC. 14 March 2003. Retrieved 19 August 2008.
32. Vijay Singh, Syed Firdaus Ashra (29 July 2003). "Blast in Ghatkopar in Mumbai, 4 killed and 32 injured". rediff.comIndia Limited. Archived

from the original on 8 September 2008. Retrieved 19 August 2008.

33. "2003: Bombay rocked by twin car bombs". BBC. 25 August 2003. Retrieved 19 August 2008.
34. "For the record: The 11/7 chargesheet". rediff.com India Limited. 11 July 2008. Retrieved 19 August 2008.
35. "India: A major terror target". The Times of India (India). 30 October 2008. Retrieved 11 November 2008.[dead link]
36. Dwight Hamilton; Kostas Rimsa (19 November 2007). Terror Threat: International and Homegrown Terrorists and Their Threat to Canada. Dundurn Press Ltd.. p. 103. ISBN 978-1-55002-736-5. Retrieved 28 September 2011.
37. "'Rs 50, 000 not enough for injured'". Indian Express Newspapers (Mumbai) Ltd.. 21 July 2006. Retrieved 11 November 2008.
38. India's 26/11: From Communal Violence to Communal Terrorism to Terrorism, Editorial, K. Jaishankar, INternational Journal of Criminal Justice Sciences, Vol 2 Issue 2 July – december 2007, 2007, (IJCJS) ISSN: 0973-5089 Vol 2 (2): 5–11
39. "India police: Pakistan spy agency behind Mumbai bombings". CNN. 1 October 2006. Retrieved 11 November 2008.
40. "Mumbai Police blames ISI, LeT for 7/11 blasts". The Times of India (India). 30 September 2006. Retrieved 11 November 2008.
41. Moreau, Ron; Mazumdar, Sudip (27 November 2008). "The Pakistan Connection". Newsweek. Archived from the original on 6 December 2008. Retrieved 28 November 2008.
42. a b "3 witnesses identify Kasab, court takes on record CCTV footage". The Economic Times (India). 17 June 2009.Archived from the original on 20 June 2009. Retrieved 17 June 2009.
43. a b "Photographer recalls Mumbai attacks". The News International. 16 June 2009. Archived from the original on 20 June 2009. Retrieved 17 June 2009.
44. Judgement, THE HIGH COURT OF JUDICATURE AT BOMBAY, THE JUDGMENT RESERVED : 7TH FEBRUARY, 2011; THE

ORDER IS PRONOUNCED: 21ST FEBRUARY, 2011.

45. "Info from cop in Karkare's jeep led to Kasab's arrest". Mid Day. 3 December 2008. Archived from the original on 17 June 2011. Retrieved 15 July 2011.
46. "Mumbai gunman guilty of 'act of war'". The National (Abu Dhabi). 4 May 2010. Retrieved 15 July 2011.
47. "Jukexboxes on the Moon: Stardom is martyrdom: India arrives in the American imagination". Triple Canopy. Retrieved 15 July 2011.
48. Blakely, Rhys; Page, Jeremy (1 December 2008). "Defiant Leopold café shows that Mumbai is not afraid". The Times(UK). Retrieved 19 March 2009.
49. "Leopold Cafe reopens amidst desolation". Deccan Herald(India). 1 December 2008. Archived from the original on 5 December 2008. Retrieved 19 March 2009.
50. "Mumbai attack: Timeline of how the terror unfolded". Daily Mirror. UK. 27 November 2008. Archived from the original on 28 May 2009. Retrieved 25 May 2009.
51. "Taj Hotel Burns, 2 Terrorists Killed". CNN IBN. 27 November 2008. Retrieved 27 November 2008.
52. "Taj Hotel Attacked". TTKN News. 27 November 2008. Retrieved 27 November 2008.
53. a b "Scores killed in Mumbai rampage". CNN. 26 November 2008. Archived from the original on 2 December 2008. Retrieved 26 November 2008.
54. Andrew Stevens, Mallika Kapur, Phil O'Sullivan, Phillip Turner, Ravi Hiranand, Yasmin Wong and Harmeet Shah Singh (27 November 2008). "Fighting reported at Mumbai Jewish center". CNN. Archived from the original on 2 December 2008. Retrieved 28 November 2008.
55. Pasricha, Anjana (27 November 2008). "Commandos Launch Operations to Clear Luxury Hotels Seized by Gunmen in Mumbai". VOA News (Voice of America). Archived from the original on 17 July 2011.
56. "We want all Mujahideen released: Terrorist inside Oberoi".The Times

of India (India). 27 November 2008. Retrieved 27 November 2008.

57. Patrick Frater (30 November 2008). "Indian journalists in media firestorm". Variety. Archived from the original on 2 December 2008. Retrieved 1 December 2008.

58. "Mumbai operation appears nearly over". CNN. 29 November 2008. Archived from the original on 8 March 2009. Retrieved 23 February 2009.

59. "Oberoi standoff ends". CNN. 28 November 2008. Archived from the original on 23 July 2011. Retrieved 7 March 2009.

60. "Terrorists had no plan to blow up Taj: NSG DG". Rediff. Retrieved 26 November 2009.[dead link]

61. "NSG commando recounts gunfight with terrorists". CNN IBN. Retrieved 26 November 2009.

62. Blakely, Rhys (22 December 2008). "A taste of defiance as massacre hotel opens for high tea". The Times (UK). Retrieved 8 January 2011.

63. Charter, David (27 November 2008). "Tory MEP flees for his life as gunman starts spraying the hotel bar with bullets". The Times (London). Retrieved 21 February 2008.

64. "EU trade delegation in Mumbai safe, delegate says".Deutsche Presse-Agentur. 27 November 2008. Retrieved 23 February 2009.

65. a b c Charter, David (27 November 2008). "Tory MEP flees for his life as gunman starts spraying the hotel bar with bullets".The Times (UK). Retrieved 27 November 2008.

66. "EU parliament staff member wounded in India shootout". EU business. 27 November 2008. Archived from the originalon 3 December 2008. Retrieved 21 February 2009.

67. MEP attacks EU consular reaction in Mumbai, PHILIPPA RUNNER, 8 December 2008 @ 17:19 CET, euobserver.com

68. "Relacja Polaka z piekła" (in Polish). Reuters, TVN24. 27 November 2008. Retrieved 21 February 2009.

69. a b "EU parliament staff member wounded in India shootout". The Times of India (India). 27 November 2008. Retrieved 21 February 2009.

70. Press Trust of India (27 November 2008). "200 people held hostage at

Taj Hotel". NDTV. Retrieved 21 February 2009.

71. Thomson, Alice; Rachel Sylvester (27 November 2008). "Sir Gulam Noon, British 'Curry King': how I escaped bombed hotel". The Times (UK). Retrieved 27 November 2008.

72. Vaakov Lappin (29 November 2008). "Consulate: Unspecified number of Israelis missing in Mumbai". Jerusalem Post. Retrieved 27 November 2008.

73. "NSG ends reign of terror at Nariman". Times of India(India). 29 November 2008. Retrieved 23 February 2009.

74. Daniel Trotta (28 November 2008). "Rabbi killed in Mumbai had gone to serve Jews". Reuters. Archived from the original on 3 December 2008. Retrieved 29 November 2008.

75. Gee, Alastair (1 November 2009), "Mumbai terror attacks: And then they came for the Jews", The Times (London), retrieved 15 July 2011[dead link]

76. Gee, Alastair, And then they came for the Jews, Samoa Observer, retrieved 15 July 2011

77. Keith Bradsher and Somini Sengupta (28 November 2008)."Commandos storm Jewish center in Mumbai". International Herald Tribune. Archived from the original on 1 December 2008. Retrieved 28 November 2008.

78. "Mumbai takes back control from terrorists". TTKN Oxford. 28 November 2008. Archived from the original on 28 December 2008. Retrieved 28 November 2008.

79. a b c "Gunbattle enters third day, intense firing at Taj hotel". 28 November 2008. Archived from the original on 1 December 2008. Retrieved 28 November 2008.

80. "Taj operation over, three terrorists killed". Hindustan Times(India). 29 November 2008. Archived from the original on 2 December 2008. Retrieved 29 November 2008.

81. "Battle for Mumbai ends, death toll rises to 195". The Times of India (India). 29 November 2008. Retrieved 21 February 2009.

82. "Timeline: one night of slaughter and mayhem". Evening Standard. 27 November 2008. Archived from the original on 5 December 2008. Retrieved 1 December 2008.

83. 27 July 2009, Jane; Masood, Salman. New York Times: p. A4.http://www.nytimes.com/2009/07/27/world/asia/27pstan.html?pagewanted=print Terror Ties Run Deep in Pakistan, Mumbai Case Shows.'

84. a b Schmitt, Eric; Sengupta, Somini (4 December 2008). "Ex-US Official Cites Pakistani Training for India Attackers". The New York Times. Retrieved 3 December 2008.

85. Hussain, Zahid (28 July 2009). "Islamabad Tells of Plot by Lashkar". Wall Street Journal (Islamabad). Retrieved 28 July 2009.

86. Schifrin, Nick (25 November 2009). "Mumbai terror attacks: 7 Pakistanis charged". ABC News. Archived from the original on 27 November 2009. Retrieved 1 December 2009.

87. Rhys Blakely (26 February 2009). "Pakistani Army colonel 'was involved' in Mumbai terror attacks". The Times (London). Retrieved 26 February 2009.

88. "Who are David Headley, Tahawwur Rana?". CNN IBN. 17 November 2009. Archived from the original on 21 November 2009. Retrieved 21 November 2009.

89. Mohan, Vishwa (7 November 2009). "Headley link traced to Pak, 2 LeT men arrested". Times of India (India). Retrieved 21 November 2009.

90. Associated Press, "Four more men charged in Mumbai attack", Japan Times, 27 April 2011, p. 4.

91. Baqir Sajjad Syed and Mohammad Asghar (9 February 2009)."Investigators see Bangladesh link in Mumbai terror attacks".Dawn. Archived from the original on 28 May 2009. Retrieved 10 February 2009.

92. "Chidambaram asserts 26/11 originated from Pak soil".The Hindu (Chennai, India). 9 February 2009. Retrieved 21 February 2009.

93. Shakeel Ahmad (16 February 2009). "Samjhota, Mumbai attacks linked, says Qureshi". Dawn. Archived from the original on 19 February 2009. Retrieved 16 February 2009.

94. a b Richard A. Oppel and Salman Masood (7 January 2009)."Gunman in Mumbai Siege a Pakistani, Official Says". The New York Times. Archived from the original on 1 March 2009. Retrieved 21 February 2009.

95. Mubashir Zaidi (7 January 2009). "Surviving gunman's identity established as Pakistani". Dawn. Archived from the original on 28 May 2009. Retrieved 7 January 2009.

96. a b "Part of 26/11 plan made on our land, admits Pakistan".NDTV. 12 February 2009. Archived from the original on 13 February 2009. Retrieved 12 February 2009.

97. Anirban Bhaumik (4 January 2009). "PC heads for US with 26/11 proof". Deccan Herald (India). Retrieved 21 February 2009.[dead link]

98. Rupert, James (28 January 2009). "Pakistan's Partial Crackdown Lets Imams Preach Jihad". Bloomberg. Retrieved 6 December 2009.

99. Praveen Swami (23 November 2009). "Missing evidence mars Mumbai massacre probe". The Hindu (Chennai, India). Retrieved 15 July 2011.

100. Reporters Without Borders (13 November 2009). "Two journalists held after helping media probe Mumbai attacker's background". Reporters Without Borders. Retrieved 15 July 2011.

101. Nirupama Subramanian (24 November 2009). "Kasab's village remains a no-go area for journalists". The Hindu(Chennai, India). Retrieved 15 July 2011.

102. PTI (1 December 2009). "No information on Headley, Rana from Pakistan, says Home Minister Chidambaram". Times of India (India). Retrieved 15 July 2011.

103. a b "Indian gov't: Pakistan spies tied to Mumbai siege".news.yahoo.com. Associated Press. 19 October 2010. Archived from the original on 21 October 2010. Retrieved 20 October 2010.

104. a b "Report: Pakistan Spies Tied to Mumbai Siege". Associated Press. Fox News. 19 October 2010. Archived from the original on 22 November 2010. Retrieved 20 October 2010.

105. "Slain navigator of Porbandar trawler was imprisoned in Pak". The Times of India (India). 30 September 2008.Archived from the original on 28 May 2009. Retrieved 15 February 2009.

106. "Terror boat was almost nabbed off Mumbai". The Times of India (India). 10 December 2008. Retrieved 17 May 2010.

107. a b New York Times, 16 Oct. 2010 "US Had Warnings on Plotter of Mumbai Attack,"http://www.nytimes.com/2010/10/17/world/asia/17headley.html?pagewanted=1&_r=1&ref=global-home

108. Pro Publica, 15 Oct. 2010 "FBI Was Warned Years in Advance of Mumbai Attacker's Terror Ties,"http://www.propublica.org/article/mumbai-plot-fbi-was-warned-years-in-advance

109. a b New York Times, 17 Dec. 2010 "Top US Spy Leaves Pakistan After His Name Is Revealed,"http://www.nytimes.com/2010/12/18/world/asia/18pstan.html?hp

110. "26/11: Abu Jundal names same Pak army officers as Headley did". 3 July 2012.

111. "26/11 had been planned originally for 2006, reveals Abu Hamza". NDTV. 26 June 2012. Retrieved 26 June 2012.

112. "26/11: Pakistan says Mumbai attackers were helped by 40 Indians". Times of India. 2 July 2012. Retrieved 2 July 2012.

113. Ali, S Ahmed (30 November 2008). "Mumbai locals helped us, terrorist tells cops". The Times of India (India). Retrieved 30 November 2008.

114. Sheela Bhatt (27 November 2008). "Exclusive: LeT terrorist Ismail arrested in Mumbai". Rediff.com. Archived from the original on 5 December 2008. Retrieved 29 November 2008.

115. Ishaan Tharoor (4 December 2008). "Pakistani Involvement in the Mumbai Attacks". TIME. Retrieved 21 February 2009.

116. Rhys Blakely (4 December 2008). "Mumbai gunman says he was paid $1,900 for attack – as new CCTV emerges". The Times (UK). Retrieved 21 February 2009.

117. "Indian 'scouted attack' in Mumbai". Herald Sun (Australia). 6 December 2008. Retrieved 21 February 2009.

118. "Two men accused of providing SIM cards to Mumbai attackers". CBC News. 6 December 2008. Archived from the original on 22 March 2009. Retrieved 21 February 2009.

119. Chang, Gordon G. (13 August 2009). "India's China Problem –". Forbes. Retrieved 31 December 2010.

120. Damien McElroy (3 December 2008). "Mumbai attacks Terrorists took cocaine to stay awake during assault". The Daily Telegraph (London). Archived from the original on 9 February 2009. Retrieved 21 February 2009.

121. Rahul Bedi (9 December 2008). "Mumbai attacks: Indian suit against Google Earth over image use by terrorists". The Daily Telegraph (London). Archived from the original on 11 February 2009. Retrieved 20 February 2009.

122. Somini Sengupta and Keith Bradsher (29 November 2008)."India Faces Reckoning as Terror Toll Eclipses 170". The New York Times. Retrieved 21 February 2009.

123. Rakesh Prakash (29 November 2008). "Please give me saline". The Times of India (India). Archived from the original on 2 March 2009. Retrieved 21 February 2009.

124. Ramesh, Randeep (28 November 2008). "They were in no hurry. Cool and composed, they killed and killed". The Guardian (UK). Archived from the original on 1 December 2008. Retrieved 29 November 2008.

125. Balakrishnan, Angela (28 November 2008). "Claims emerge of British terrorists in Mumbai". The Guardian (London). Retrieved 29 November 2008, UK.

126. Tom Morgan (28 November 2008). "Arrested Mumbai gunmen 'of British descent'". The Independent (UK). Archived from the original on 1 December 2008. Retrieved 28 November 2008.

127. Jon Swaine (28 November 2008). "Mumbai attack: Government 'has no evidence of British involvement'". The Daily Telegraph (London). Archived from the original on 2 February 2009. Retrieved 28 February 2009.

128. McElroy, Damien (6 Dec 2008). "Mumbai attacks: police admit there were more than ten attackers". The Daily Telegraph(London). Retrieved 4 Aug 2009.

129. Jeremy Kahn and Robert F. Worth (9 December 2008)."Mumbai Attackers Called Part of Larger Band of Recruits". The New York Times. Retrieved 21 February 2009.

130. Bodies of nine Mumbai gunmen buried secretly in JanReuters, Tue 6 Apr 2010 10:26 pm IST

131. Swami, Praveen (2008-12-92). "A journey into the Lashkar".The Hindu (Chennai, India). Archived from the original on 5 December 2008. Retrieved 5 December 2008.

132. "Planned 9/11 at Taj, reveals caught terrorist". Zee News. 29 November 2008. Retrieved 21 February 2009.

133. Kamran Haider (12 February 2009). "Pakistan says it arrests Mumbai attack plotters". Reuters. Archived from the originalon 2012-06-25. Retrieved 26 June 2012.

134. "Italy arrests two for Mumbai attacks". The Hindu (India). 21 November 2009. Retrieved 21 November 2009.[dead link]

135. "Two Pakistanis arrested in connection with Mumbai attacks". France 24. 21 November 2009. Retrieved 14 August 2011.

136. "Pak mum on 26/11 terror duo held in Italy". The Times of India. India. Retrieved 1 September 2011.

137. "Mumbai police probe David Headley's links to 26/11 attacks". Daily News and Analysis (India). 8 November 2009.Archived from the original on 16 November 2009. Retrieved 16 November 2009.

138. "India Plans to Try Chicago Man For Mumbai Attacks". Reuters. 8 December 2009. Retrieved 15 July 2011.[dead link]

139. Josy Joseph (9 November 2009). "David Headley posed as Jew in Mumbai". Daily News and Analysis (India). Archivedfrom the original on 12 November 2009. Retrieved 16 November 2009.

140. ET Bureau (9 December 2009). "FBI nails Pak Major for Mumbai attacks". India Times. Retrieved 9 December 2009.

141. 26/11 attacks handler arrested Hindustan Times, Abhishek Sharan & Ashok Das, Delhi/Hyderabad, 18 January 2010

142. "Key 26/11 conspirator Abu Hamza arrested at IGI airport in Delhi". IBN Live. 25 June 2012. Retrieved 25 June 2012.

143. "Key Mumbai terror attack handler arrested in Delhi". 25 June 2012.

144. "Key 26/11 terrorist arrested". The Hindu. 25 June 2012. Retrieved

25 June 2012.

145. http://ibnlive.in.com/news/2611-suspect-abu-jindal-in-delhi-police-net/267804-3.html

146. "Pakistan used cricket diplomacy to survey terror targets". 30 June 2012.

147. "Jundal had a very safe haven in Pakistan: Chidambaram". 29 June 2012.

148. "Maharashtra minister denies links with Jundal, says ready for probe". 26 June 2012.

149. "Indian forces storm Jewish centre". BBC News. 27 November 2008. Archived from the original on 28 November 2008. Retrieved 27 November 2008.

150. "One Japanese killed, another wounded in Mumbai shootings". Channel NewsAsia. Archived from the original on 3 December 2008. Retrieved 26 November 2008.

151. P.S. Suryanarayana (27 November 2008). "Caught in the crossfire, 9 foreign nationals killed". The Hindu (Chennai, India). Retrieved 27 November 2008.

152. Stevens, Andrew; Mallika Kapur, Harmeet Shah Singh, Saeed Ahmed, Sara Sidner, Alessio Vinci, Reza Sayah, Paula Newton(29 November 2008). "Indian official: Terrorists wanted to kill 5,000". CNN. Archived from the original on 2 December 2008. Retrieved 30 November 2008.

153. Krishnakumar P and Vicky Nanjappa (30 November 2008)."Rediff: Doctors shocked at hostages's torture". Rediff.com.Archived from the original on 5 March 2009. Retrieved 21 February 2009.

154. Naughton, Philippe (27 November 2008). "British yachting tycoon Andreas Liveras killed in Bombay terror attacks". The Times (UK). Retrieved 27 November 2008.

155. "Three top cops die on duty". The Times of India (India). 27 November 2008. Retrieved 27 November 2008.

156. "Indian victims include financier, journalist, actor's sister, police". CNN. 30 November 2008. Archived from the original on 2 December 2008. Retrieved 30 November 2008.

157. "Key developments in Mumbai terror attacks". The Hindu(India). 27

Retrieved 15 July 2011.

183. Chamberlain, Gethin (3 May 2010). "Mumbai gunman convicted of murder over terror attacks". The Guardian(London). Archived from the original on 6 May 2010. Retrieved 3 May 2010.
184. Deshpande, Swati (3 May 2010). "26/11 Kasab held guilty 2 Indians walk free". The Times of India. Retrieved 4 May 2010.
185. "Indian Supreme Court upholds death penalty for Kasab".AFP. Dawn. 29 August 2012. Retrieved 29 August 2012.
186. Officials Fear New Mumbai-Style Attack, Lydia Polgreen and Souad Mekhennet, New York Times, 30 September 2009
187. Fareed Zakaria, transcript of CNN interview with Manmohan Singh (23 Nov 2009). "Pakistan has not done enough on attacks". Wall Street Journal. Retrieved 15 July 2011.
188. "26/11 trial: Pak court reserves decision on Lakhvi plea". 14 July 2012.
189. "Mumbai terror attacks: Pak court calls judicial panel's report illegal". 17 July 2012.
190. "26/11: Upset over Pak court ruling, India says will talk to govt". 17 July 2012.
191. "Pakistan asks India to allow 2nd visit of its 26/11 commission". 2012-08-08.
192. How Oberoi hotel accidentally became a 26/11 target, 15 June 2011 17:06 IST, rediff.com
193. "Rana acquitted on terror plot". Deccan Herald. Retrieved 16 Jun 2011.
194. "Mumbai bustles but also remembers 26/11 victims". CNN IBN. Archived from the original on 29 November 2009. Retrieved 26 November 2009.
195. "India remembers Mumbai dead". CNN. 26 November 2010. Retrieved 31 December 2010.
196. "City's first flashmob entertains commuters at CST".Hindustan Times. India. Retrieved 29 November 2011.
197. "Mumbai's first flash mob at CST surprises all". CNN-IBN. 29 November 2011. Retrieved 29 November 2011.

About IISSM

The International Institute of Security and Safety Management (IISSM) is a non-profit educational organization. It is devoted towards promoting professionalism among security and loss prevention practitioners and creating all round security awareness and consciousness amongst personnel in the related management cadre. It offers consultancy services and runs customised and thematic courses covering all aspects of industrial security, safety, fire prevention, loss prevention and allied subjects. It acts as a catalyst to bring professionals together for experience-sharing and updating professional knowledge through numerous training courses, seminars and workshops. It has an elaborated Professional Certification Programme for security and safety practitioners and consultants and bestows Fellowship on highly selected professionals.

It has been organising International Seminars, at times

accompanied by Exhibitions, every year since 1991 attracting a large number of security and loss prevention professionals from India and abroad. Faculties in these Seminars comprise of well-known experts drawn from all over the world. Participants come from private sector industries, public sector undertakings, private security agencies, systems integrators, security equipment manufacturers, academic institutions, financial institutions and banking industries as well as departments and ministries of the government. Countries so far represented in IISSM Training Programms are: Australia, Bangladesh, Belgium, Canada, Denmark, France, Germany, Hong Kong, Special Administrative Region, Indonesia, Israel, Kuwait, Malaysia, Mauritius, Mozambique, Nepal, Reunion Island, Saudi Arabia, Singapore, South Africa, Taiwan, Province of China, Thailand, Turkey, UK, USA, Zambia, Zimbabwe, India.

IISSM offers membership to professionals from safety, security, risk and disaster management, security officers, managers and other total loss prevention professionals. Please refer to the Membership details for enrolling as a member.

For more information on IISSM, please visit www.iissm.com

***